# Visions of Washington Irving

## SELECTED WORKS FROM THE COLLECTIONS OF HISTORIC HUDSON VALLEY

Engᵈ by W. Kinson.

# Visions of Washington Irving

SELECTED WORKS FROM THE COLLECTIONS OF

HISTORIC HUDSON VALLEY

Historic
Hudson
Valley

EXHIBITION SCHEDULE
Federal Hall National Memorial
New York City
October 2–December 31, 1991

Hudson River Museum of Westchester
Yonkers, New York
February 7–June 21, 1992

New York State Museum
Albany, New York
July 17–September 6, 1992

This exhibition was supported in part by a grant from the
National Endowment for the Arts, a federal agency.

Historic Hudson Valley
150 White Plains Road
Tarrytown, NY 10591

Library of Congress Card Catalog No.: 91-75568

ISBN: 0-912882-99-9

COVER: *Washington Irving and His Literary Friends at Sunnyside*,
by Christian Schussele, cat. no. 12.

HALF-TITLE: *Sunnyside*, from Benson Lossing's *The Hudson from the Wilderness
to the Sea*, Troy, NY: H.B Nims & Co., 1866.

TITLE: *The Author of the Sketch-Book*, engraving by William Keenan
(c. 1810–1855), published by E. Littell, Philadelphia, c. 1820.

*Visions of Washington Irving*
was produced for Historic Hudson Valley
by Perpetua Press, Los Angeles.
Edited by Letitia Burns O'Connor
Designed by Dana Levy
Typeset by Continental Typographics
    in Stempel Garamond
Printed by South China Printing Co.
Manufactured in Hong Kong

# Contents

Sunnyside, 1988

# Preface

"VISIONS OF WASHINGTON IRVING: Selected Works from the Collections of Historic Hudson Valley" honors Washington Irving and his house, Sunnyside, as focal points of America's artistic life during the first half of the nineteenth century.

Washington Irving was a celebrity in his time, an upstart writer from America who captured the imagination of his countrymen and of the literary lions of England, not long after a British critic had asked "Who reads an American book?"

Irving, whose colorful and painterly style continues to delight readers here and abroad, had a profound influence on the artists of his day, providing many of them with themes, inspiration, and lasting friendship.

"I thank God I was born on the banks of the Hudson!" he wrote in 1839. And he returned to the Hudson to create his beloved Sunnyside, itself an extraordinary artistic statement of the time.

Historic Hudson Valley has organized "Visions of Washington Irving" in celebration of our fortieth anniversary. The exhibition provides a splendid vehicle to reacquaint the public with Washington Irving and his world.

Most of the paintings in this exhibition were purchased for us by Mrs. John D. Rockefeller, Jr. in 1946 and have not, as a group, previously been on public view. What better way to introduce this body of work than through a thoughtful exhibition and catalog.

Thanks go to David M. Sokol for his fine essay. The entries in the catalog were prepared by Kathleen Eagen Johnson, registrar and librarian, and James Archer Abbott, assistant curator. Their initials stand as signatures of their research, the backbone of the exhibition.

Joseph T. Butler, curator and director of museum operations, supervised this project and thanks go to him and his fine staff.

"Visions of Washington Irving" has been made possible through generous grants from the National Endowment for the Arts and the J. M. Kaplan Fund, Inc., for which we are most appreciative.

JOHN H. DOBKIN
President
Historic Hudson Valley

# Washington Irving:

## SQUIRE OF SUNNYSIDE

BY JOSEPH T. BUTLER

WASHINGTON IRVING (1783–1859) was one of America's early ambassadors of style and taste. He brought understanding of America to Europe and introduced many Americans to aspects of European culture. He stands today as an important representative of the new nation's artistic creativity at the turn of the nineteenth century.

Born in New York City during the last weeks of the American Revolution, this youngest of eight surviving children of Scottish immigrants was named in honor of the war's greatest hero, General George Washington. In later years Irving was fond of telling that, as a child, he was introduced to Washington in a New York City shop and received a presidential pat on his then-curly head.

Over the course of his long life, Irving had many more occasions to meet famous people. Such literary giants as Sir Walter Scott, Henry Wadsworth Longfellow, and Charles Dickens heaped praise upon the first genuinely American author. Such artists as David Wilkie, Gilbert Stuart Newton, and Felix O. C. Darley vied for the chance to capture his visage or his fanciful characters in pencil or on canvas. (Irving's lifelong relationships with artists are amply covered in David Sokol's essay, "Washington Irving: Friend and Muse to American Artists.")

Traveling widely, Irving befriended people everywhere, from presidents and kings to village neighbors and children, and became one of America's most beloved and respected citizens. Honors bestowed upon him during his lifetime confirm the high regard in which he was held by his contemporaries. He received honorary degrees from Columbia University (A.M. 1821, LL.D. 1829), from Harvard University (LL.D. 1832), and from Oxford University (D.C.L. 1831).

Spain elected Irving to membership in the Real Academia de La Historia (1828), and England's Royal Society of Literature voted him its prized Gold Medal in History (1830). He declined an offer from the Tammany Society to run for Mayor of the City of New York in 1838, but he did serve for ten years as the first president of the Astor Library, forerunner

Irving's Voltaire chair in his study, Sunnyside, palladium print, 1991.

9

*The Chieftain and the Child*, watercolor by George B. Butler, 1854. President George Washington pats the head of his young namesake, Washington Irving.

of the New York Public Library. In 1849 the Smithsonian Institution elected Irving an honorary member, one of very few such in the long history of that prestigious organization.

Although he trained for the law and tried his hand at the family business, Irving achieved fame as a writer. He gained recognition as a humorist with the publication in 1809 of *Diedrich Knickerbocker's A History of New-York*, a satirical and still very amusing account of the early Dutch settlers of Manhattan. Irving's fictitious historian, Diedrich Knickerbocker, gained such popularity that the word "Knickerbocker" soon came to mean "New Yorker."

It was *The Sketch-Book*, however, that earned international acclaim for this New York author. Published in 1819–1820, while Irving was living in England, *The Sketch-Book* contained vivid descriptions of English Christmas customs and was largely responsible for popularizing those traditions in this country. The book also introduced Irving's famous Hudson River Valley characters: the Headless Horseman, who chased Ichabod Crane over the hills of Tarrytown, and Rip Van Winkle, who slept through the entire Revolutionary War, high in the Catskill Mountains.

Irving was fascinated by Spain, where he spent many years perfecting his command of the language, doing research, and traveling extensively. His experiences there resulted in *The Life and Voyages of Christopher Columbus* (1828), the first English biography of the great explorer, and *The Alhambra* (1832), a fascinating series of sketches based on this medieval fortified palace built by the Moorish ruler of Granada.

During the seventeen years Irving spent living and writing in Europe (1815–1832), he served in the diplomatic corps in London as Secretary to the American Legation at the Court of St. James, as well as attempting to save his family's export business in Liverpool. When he returned to New York in 1832, he wondered how he might be received by his countrymen after such a long absence. He need not have worried, for New York greeted him with a huge testimonial dinner at which he was the toast of the town.

Wishing to get back in touch with his own country, Irving joined a U.S. Army expedition to the West, traveling by horseback to what was then the Oklahoma Territory. From this adventure flowed *A Tour on the Prairies* (1835) in which he described riding after a herd of buffalo and downing one with a single shot. His friendship with John Jacob Astor led to the publication of *Astoria* (1836), a history of Astor's fur-trading ventures in the Pacific Northwest.

Having lived out of a suitcase for most of his adult life, Washington Irving longed for a place he could truly call home. In 1835 he returned to the area he had made famous in "The Legend of Sleepy Hollow" and purchased a small Dutch farmhouse beside the Hudson River in Tarrytown, New York. The stone cottage, built in the latter years of the seventeenth century, was a rectangular, boxlike structure with a pitched roof. Assisted by his neighbor, landscape painter George Harvey, Irving created a romantic retreat he lovingly called "Sunnyside," adding Dutch stepped gables of the type he had known as a boy in "New Amsterdam" and weathervanes from old buildings in New York City and Albany. Harvey had made a watercolor of the original house in 1835, which he called *The Old Cottage Taken Previous to Improvement*. About 1837 he did another watercolor, with subsequent lithograph, which he called *The Van Tassel House–the Residence of Washington Irving*. In it the house has the true romantic look with which it has since been associated. In 1847, ten years after the completion of the first remodeling of Sunnyside, he added a tower that allowed more space. Called the "Pagoda" by his friends, its design source lay in the Spanish monastery towers quite familiar to Irving from his years in Spain.

Irving was enticed away from the comforts and delights of his "snuggery" when in 1842 President John Tyler appointed him Envoy Extraordinary and Minister Plenipotentiary to the Court of Queen Isabella II of Spain. He served in this post with distinction for four years, sending entertaining dispatches home to Secretary of State Daniel Webster.

The last decade of Washington Irving's life was devoted to the completion of what he considered his greatest triumph, a five-volume biography of George Washington. *The Life of George Washington* (1855–

*The Pond*, from Benson Lossing's *The Hudson from the Wilderness to the Sea*, Troy, NY: H.B. Nims & Co., 1866.

1859) stood well into this century as the definitive work on our nation's first president.

Although Irving was a bachelor, he had several relatives living with him and frequent guests kept Sunnyside filled to capacity. His personal and literary popularity drew a steady stream of visitors to Sunnyside, who came just to shake his hand or to spend a few minutes in conversation. By the time he died on November 28, 1859, both the man and his house had become national icons.

Many who visited Sunnyside wrote their impressions or sketched the property, including Irving's neighbor Evie A. Todd, artist Benson Lossing, and illustrator Felix O. C. Darley. This extremely valuable source material has been used to document room treatment and placement of individual objects within the house, as well as providing guidance for landscape design.

The furnishings at Sunnyside, most of which are of American manufacture, date from the late eighteenth century to the middle of the nineteenth century. There are a few earlier objects of antiquarian value that Irving collected, as well as English and French silver purchased during his European sojourns. The thoroughly comfortable interiors reflect Irving's domestic happiness at Sunnyside. While it is not a house filled with grand or important furnishings, the mixture of objects representing his international travels and his many friendships reflects the genial nature of the man.

*Irving's Study*, from Benson Lossing's *The Hudson from the Wilderness to the Sea*, Troy, NY: H.B. Nims & Co., 1866.

The landscape remains much as Irving and his guests enjoyed it: rolling lawns, wildflowers gracing the banks of the stream, ducks on the pond he created and called his "Little Mediterranean," and the ever-present Hudson, flowing swiftly past on its way to meet the sea at New York harbor. Sunnyside was the home of collateral Irving descendants well into the twentieth century. In 1945 the property was acquired by the Sealantic Fund, Inc., a private philanthropy established by John D. Rockefeller, Jr., and opened to the public as a historic site in 1947.

## Historic Hudson Valley

Historic Hudson Valley (originally called Sleepy Hollow Restorations) was founded by John D. Rockefeller, Jr., and chartered by the State of New York as an educational institution in 1951. Today, the organization administers five historic properties in New York's Hudson River Valley: Philipsburg Manor, Upper Mills, at North Tarrytown; Van Cortlandt Manor at Croton-on-Hudson; Sunnyside at Tarrytown; the Union Church of Pocantico Hills at North Tarrytown; and Montgomery Place at Annandale-on-Hudson. Historic Hudson Valley also presents exhibitions and educational programs, in cooperation with the National Park Service, at Federal Hall National Memorial in New York City.

*Headless Horseman in Pursuit of Ichabod Crane,* designed and etched
by Felix O.C. Darley, published by *The American Art-Union*, 1849.

# Washington Irving:

## FRIEND AND MUSE
## TO AMERICAN ARTISTS

By David M. Sokol
Professor, History of Art and Architecture Department,
University of Illinois at Chicago

WASHINGTON IRVING (1783–1859), recognized as the "Father of American Literature" from his early adulthood to the present day, was respected and admired not only in his native land but almost as much so in Europe. Not until well after the Civil War did another American writer, Mark Twain (Samuel Clemens, 1835–1910), come to symbolize American literature to the European reading public as Washington Irving had in the first half of the century.

While Irving's fame is centered in the two most famous short stories in *The Sketch-Book* (1819), "Rip Van Winkle" and "The Legend of Sleepy Hollow," *Diedrich Knickerbocker's A History of New-York* (1809) and several of his other writings are known to a more limited audience; the rest are commonly read today only by students of American civilization. The author's complex early career as a lawyer, his involvement in a family import business, and even his years as a presidentially appointed diplomat, are long forgotten.[1] Yet, through those experiences and his consequent frequent travels and extended sojourns in Europe, Irving's personal circle of friends and colleagues was one of the widest and most diverse in America during the first half of the nineteenth century. While such contemporary authors as James Fenimore Cooper (1789–1851) and William Cullen Bryant (1794–1878) had many friends among literary, artistic, and even political figures, Irving's circle was not only more diverse but also more deeply rooted on two continents.

Other writers have discussed Irving's literary circle, his part in the New York critical and theatrical world, his friendship with noted European literary figures, including Sir Walter Scott, and even the way he utilized images of art and artists in his writing.[2] This essay concentrates on the range and depth of Irving's friendships with artists and notes the immense popularity of his writings as the source of artistic inspiration for American painters and graphic artists.[3] Painters who were his close friends as well as artists completely unknown to him exhibited major canvases based on his more popular writings, but Irving did not acquire many of these works. He was not an avid collector, more haphazard than systematic even while accumulating a large library. He did, however, receive some sketches and designs for book illustrations from several artists he befriended in Europe.

While still a youngster, Irving had been exposed to the work of several artists with connections to his large family and had taken drawing lessons at the Columbian Academy near his home, which was under the direction of Alexander and Archibald Robertson. It is not clear whether he participated in classes or had private lessons, but there is little doubt that the instruction was meant to provide a polite accomplishment rather than the start of a professional career.[4] Although he briefly flirted with the idea of becoming a painter when he first met Washington Allston, in Rome in 1805, Irving was to confine his personal artistic ventures to quick sketches of people and places he encountered. The writer's diaries and notebooks, rather than the artist's sketchbook, were the pages on which he recorded those images. Irving was content with his amateur status in the visual arts, but the writer derived great pleasure from exercising his drawing skills. He later noted: "Drawing is a delightful as well as a Gentlemanly accomplishment. The command it gives a person over his time is inconceivable. It has the power of amusing in sickness—rendering home agreeable—and beguiling a heavy hour of its heaviness."[5]

Irving was twenty-one years old when he met Washington Allston (1779–1843), and though he had already gotten to know several New York artists during his youth, being on his own and selecting his companions in each European city that he visited intensified the depth of these relationships. Allston was not only the first artist whom Irving came to know well, he was the one whom he most admired and respected for both his art and his ability to inspire. His regard for the older artist may have been influenced by appreciation of Allston's flattering suggestion that Irving had the talent to pursue a career as an artist. Indeed, Allston offered not only to instruct him in the craft of painting but also to share a studio with him, and Irving was to remember that offer with particular warmth throughout his life. Writing a reminiscence of their first meeting, Irving later recalled: "We visited together some of the finest collections of paintings and he taught me how to visit them to the most advantage; guiding me always to the master pieces, and passing by the others without notice."[6] The two spent many days together, and by the time they went their separate ways, the young writer had learned how to examine and enjoy painting, sculpture, and architecture, having been introduced to the sculpture of Michelangelo and such great buildings as St. Peters.

For the rest of his life, Irving was to write about and record his reactions to individual works of art, whether those of his fellow countrymen and friends or paintings by European masters he admired and treasured as his personal discoveries. Yet, as often as he presented his dislikes and his admiration openly, he was wont to offer a disclaimer, as he protested when venturing his opinion about some recent paintings by his British friend David Wilkie (1785–1841) in 1829, "I do not profess to be a critic in the art."[7]

When Irving left Rome for Paris, in the spring of 1805, he met and shared almost daily companionship with another young American artist, John Vanderlyn (1775–1852), with whom he had much in common. The artist was a close friend of Allston as well as being the protegé of Aaron Burr (with whom Irving would spend some time in Richmond, Virginia, during the former Vice-President's trial just two years later). Irving and Vanderlyn had both studied at the Columbian Academy and both enjoyed the theater. When Burr became unable to continue to support Vanderlyn, the artist was pressed financially, and Irving provided a modest commission in the form of a portrait sketch. Although their paths were to cross occasionally thereafter, Irving's increasing interest and presence in England and Vanderlyn's commitment to France prevented the kind of closeness that the former was to enjoy with Allston, other American painters, and his future Anglo-American friends.

When he returned home in March 1806, Irving pursued his career in law and spent a lot of his time in travel. He frequently visited northern east coast cities in regard to his family hardware business, and even ventured as far south as Richmond. He met both young and established artists in each city, becoming friends with Thomas Sully (1783–1872) and William Dunlap (1766–1839), as well as visiting the older and more established painter, John Wesley Jarvis (1780–1840). Jarvis did an oil portrait of the young writer, which, along with Vanderlyn's work, may have inspired Irving to think about building a collection. A letter written after his meeting in 1810 with the miniaturist Anson Dickinson (1779–1852) seems to support that conclusion, as he wrote, "How I would glory in being a man of opulence, to take such young artists by the hand, and cherish their budding genius."[8] But either youthful enthusiasm faded or, more likely, his expenses on travel and social obligations (combined with a knack for making bad investments) prevented him from following that particular dream. Considering the help and introductions he provided for young artists and the intensity of Irving's relationships with some of his painter friends, it is surprising that he acquired far fewer works than did such peers as William Cullen Bryant and James F. Cooper. These writers, who had also friends among the artists of the day, each acquired a substantial number of works of art. Cooper purchased and commissioned paintings from Samuel Morse (1791–1872), Thomas Cole (1801–1848), and John G. Chapman (1808–1889), and sculpture from Horatio Greenough (1805–1852). Bryant, who outlived most of his contemporaries among the Knickerbockers and was far more active in artists' associations than Irving, purchased only a few works, but was the recipient of a portfolio of over forty drawings, oils, and watercolors presented to him on his seventieth birthday. He also received gifts from artist Robert Weir (1803–1889) and the portraitist and inventor of the paint tube, John Rand. Irving's admiration for art never turned into the same sort of patronage.

Upon Irving's return from his first European visit, he settled into reading law with Judge Josiah Hoffman. The young man had a distaste for

*Diedrich Knickerbocker*, wash drawing by Felix O.C. Darley, published as frontispiece illustration for [Irving] *Diedrich Knickerbocker's A History of New-York*, New York: G.P. Putnam, 1849.

pursuing a career in the law, in which he was working as a clerk, but he continued that work as a respectable way of earning a living and as a condition of obtaining the hand of his employer's daughter, Matilda Hoffman, the object of his affections. When Matilda died tragically from tuberculosis in April 1809, Irving abandoned the field of law and concentrated on and, indeed, buried himself in, his writing. The result of his rekindled creative drive was the popular and financially successful *Diedrich Knickerbocker's A History of New-York*. He spent much time with artist friends like Sully over the next few years, even during the period of the War of 1812 in which he served as an aide-de-camp to Major General Tompkins, before beginning a seventeen-year European period rich in new artistic associations.

When Irving first returned to England in 1815, he intended to travel and perhaps seek subjects and inspiration for his writing. Within a few months of his arrival, however, he settled in Liverpool: his brother Peter was ill, and a family member was needed to look after the English branch of the family hardware firm and work on its tortured finances. Thus Irving began two years of unwanted business activity, ending with the bankruptcy of the firm. His only relief during that period came from visits to his sister Sarah, an expatriate living with her family in Birmingham. Time and again in later years when he needed a rest, her home became his place of refuge. With his stint in the business world behind him but reduced by circumstances to earning his own living, Irving thought about producing a revised and illustrated edition of the so-called Knickerbocker history, as well as starting work on another group of short stories. He began to study German, having been introduced to the richness of German folk traditions, and spent some time during the summer of 1817 at the home of Sir Walter Scott (1771–1832). After some travel through Holland, he returned to London in the summer of 1818 and once again found companionship among a circle of artists.

Washington Allston, who had been in England for a number of years, returned to America soon after the old friends became reunited in London, so correspondence was their primary form of contact for the rest of their lives. Before Allston left Europe in 1818, however, Irving asked him to produce an illustration for the projected new edition of *Diedrich Knicker-bocker's A History of New-York*. Allston introduced Irving to two young expatriate American painters who became his intimate friends, Charles Leslie (1794–1859) and Gilbert Stuart Newton (1794–1835).[9] (See cat. no. 17 for a self-portrait by Leslie.) Each of the artists was to comment on and make suggestions about Irving's writings, and he, in turn, often wrote to and about the artists and their paintings. Irving suggested particular literary and historical subjects that he thought would appeal to a British audience and commented on matters of color, composition, and style in the completed works. When Dunlap first compiled his biographical volumes, *History of the Arts of Design in the United States*, in 1834, Irving wrote the entries on Newton, Leslie, and a more recent friend, the now-forgotten pupil of his old friend Sully, William West (1788–1857).[10]

Irving, Leslie, and Newton were an active trio in the London social scene and boosted each other's careers at every possible turn. Newton, who was less theoretically oriented and, probably, less intellectual, did not have the same impact on Irving's work as did Leslie, yet he was a close social companion.[11] Neither surviving works nor artistic records suggest that Newton ever illustrated any of Irving's writings, but he did paint Irving's portrait (cat. no. 20). A portrait of Irving is also attributed to Leslie (cat. no. 18), who also produced several illustrations for the revised edition of *Diedrich Knickerbocker's A History of New-York*. Leslie, whom Irving often importuned to produce other illustrations, remained a constant source of friendly criticism and inspiration for the writer as long as he lived. Irving's ability to use words to "sketch" and Leslie's interest in working with genre images may have brought the two of them together. The proof of the considerable importance of Leslie to Irving was clearly stated in a letter

Stereoscopic slide showing Washington Irving seated in the entryway at Sunnyside, 1856.

concerning projected designs for "Bracebridge Hall," "I would rather have the work illustrated by you than anyone else."[12]

The financial success of Irving's more recent writings, especially *The Sketch-Book*, enabled him to travel to several European countries he had not yet visited. He not only explored eastern Germany but also Austria and Czechoslovakia, making extended notes on the architecture and art collections that he saw either by chance or plan. On his return from Eastern Europe in the summer of 1823, he ended up in Paris, where he met several English painters. On another visit there, the following summer, he re-encountered the American portraitist Chester Harding (1792–1866) and became close friends with William E. West. West's studio became Irving's favorite hangout in Paris, where he enjoyed meeting and conversing with artist friends. Perhaps because of his earlier flirtation with the idea of becoming a painter, the writer always valued opportunities for associating with artists and relished being asked to comment on their ideas and plans for individual works. Irving's natural sociability, his interest in art, and his thrill at being accepted by artists, though a nonprofessional, is evident by his letters, his diary entries, and the sheer amount of time he spent in the company of painters.[13]

On this same trip in 1825, Irving met the only other painter who was to vie with Allston, Leslie, and Newton for his closest affection, the British genre painter David Wilkie. Though the two men had close artistic, social, and personal dealings, the focus of this essay on Irving's American circle and his influence on American art causes us merely to note his importance in the writer's life. The importance and the intensity of this relationship characterized the next several years, particularly during Irving's first period of diplomatic service in Spain, 1826–1829, and England, 1829–1832. During those years, Newton, Leslie, and Wilkie were also in close contact with Irving's friend and mentor, Sir Walter Scott, about illustrations of his novels. (See cat. no. 16 for a portrait of Scott by Newton.)

When he returned to the United States in the spring of 1832, Irving continued the relationship with his artist friends with both words and deeds. For example, the glowing and appreciative accounts of Newton, Leslie, and West that he provided for the previously mentioned work by Dunlap were more than biographies, causing Leslie to demur that "you have said much more for me than I deserve."[14] Irving showed his affection for Wilkie, which was based on their shared experiences in Spain several years earlier, by dedicating his next book, *The Alhambra*, to him. Yet he was (and remained) closest to Leslie. He encouraged his friend to revisit the country of his birth and suggested that he might enjoy a visit to the American West. He even suggested the possibility of helping Leslie obtain an assignment as the official artist on an expedition, to cover the cost of the trip. When Leslie was invited to be professor of drawing at West Point, Irving scrupulously pointed out the pros and cons, while firmly expressing his personal pleasure at the thought of their possible proximity. Leslie did accept the position, but remained in it—and in the United States—for less than one year. He then returned to London at the end of the 1834 spring term after a farewell party at the National Academy of Design, which was attended by Irving and his other artist friends.

Irving spent the decade following his return to America traveling and writing as busily as ever. He often saw Dunlap in New York, and occasionally visited with Newton, now settled in Boston, and William West, who returned to New York in 1840. He also made new friends among the artistic community, including John J. Audubon (1785–1851), but the new acquaintance who became his closest associate was the English painter and architect George Harvey, (c. 1800–1878). Irving relied on the younger man through the stages of remodelling, design, and construction of the home that became known as Sunnyside.[14] These two men were able to discuss theory and the relationship of the building to its setting because of a shared English experience, Harvey native to England and Irving so long a resident in that country and familiar with its customs and values. Harvey's own watercolor paintings (cat. nos. 44 and 46) are based on the British nineteenth-century landscape tradition and illustrate the Englishman's interest in the placement of the home in a picturesque setting. An appreciation of coziness and domesticity, equally far from the wilds of nature and the confines of the city, mark the two men's approach to and appreciation of domestic architecture and the proper life for a gentleman. With the exception of Harvey, who was not a professional full-time artist in the mold of Allston, Wilkie, or Leslie, Irving never again had a close personal relationship with an artist. When he returned to America from his seventeen-year absence, despite his election in 1841 as an Honorary Member of the National

Academy of Design, Irving never again found a circle of artist friends. Unlike Bryant or such Knickerbocker writers as Gulian Verplanck (1786–1870) and Charles F. Hoffman (1806–1884), Irving neither joined The Sketch Club nor followed the lead of Morse or Weir in journeying to the city to participate in its affairs. Thus, in spite of numerous opportunities for sustained relationships with Cole, Durand, Kensett (1816–1872), and the other Hudson River landscape painters, and with such narrative painters as Daniel Huntington (1816–1906), Francis W. Edmonds (1806–1863), and Morse, Irving evidently preferred to confine his contact to letters and occasional meetings.

Irving's last European interlude was spent in Spain, where he served as the American Minister—Envoy Extraordinary and Minister Plenipotentiary—from 1842 to 1846. He visited with Leslie, his remaining artist friend in England, when the writer/diplomat spent a few weeks in London on his way to take up his post in Madrid. Their reunion was a warm one, although the social requirements of Irving's job limited their meetings to only a few. Irving was delighted to see that the expatriate painter was so successful, receiving royal commissions and many others to take up as time permitted. After a similarly brief visit to Paris, Irving was off to Spain.

Irving's responsibilities as Envoy Extraordinary and Minister Plenipotentiary far exceeded those of his prior role as an attaché and left him less opportunity for travel. Further, with many of his old friends gone, he had no one to share his enthusiasms as he had in the past, but he kept abreast of developments in the New York art world through letters sent by his life-long friend, Henry Brevoort (1791–1874). Brevoort introduced him to a young American artist, William H. Powell (1823–1879), who was planning to study Spanish painting, and Irving apparently directed him to those collections he thought most important. Although Powell never became a close friend of the writer, Irving seems to have thought very highly of his abilities. His show of personal support, so often given to his earlier artist friends, was now extended to the young Powell. At the death of Henry Inman (1801–1846), who had been working on one of the last four panels for the rotunda of the United States Capitol (and was the creator of several other paintings based on Irving subjects), Powell sought and received Irving's support to replace Inman in that very prestigious commission.[16]

The commission was desirable for its $10,000 fee, but the fame and visibility of such a work would be worth far more to the winning artist. Consequently, many artists vied for the prize, including Inman's own pupil, Daniel Huntington (1816–1906), who later based a canvas on an Irving subject (see cat. no. 34). The commission was awarded to the twenty-four-year-old Powell, whose application had been supported by a letter from Irving to the Congressional Committee on Public Buildings, the body responsible for the selection of artists to produce the eight panels. Many other influential citizens wrote in support of other artists, but the advice and recommendation of the recently retired American minister, who was known to be quite involved with artists, seems to have carried a lot of weight.[17]

Drawing after Felix O.C. Darley, used as frontispiece
for *The Alhambra*, New York: G.P. Putnam, 1851.

Powell and Irving remained in contact after the artist completed his rotunda panel, and the writer/diplomat provided him with valuable introductions to people who could be of help when the young artist moved to Paris to fulfill his contract. Powell later produced at least two portraits of the writer: the first, a small watercolor on ivory (cat. no. 50) and later, a life-size post-humous painting which was the source for a popular engraving.

Irving never again enjoyed sustained contact with artists as he had with the friends of his young adulthood and never had an impact on a career like he had on young Powell, but his relationship to the art world remained both active and important. In the last decade of his life he met other artists, including Felix Darley (1822–1888), Emanuel Leutze (1816–1868), and Charles Loring Elliott (1812–1868) and often invited younger artists (including Elliott, whose work he admired) to visit him at Sunnyside. He also had the opportunity of having his portrait painted by many of the best contemporary and older artists, but he seems to have declined all such requests. Elliott, in particular, was much sought after as a portraitist, as was the much older Samuel Waldo (1783–1861), and each approached the highly regarded author with flattering offers to paint his portrait. Each invitation was rejected in turn, always with the explanation that, having declined to sit for others, he could not make an exception that would lead to bad feelings among those whose offers he had rejected. The lone exception was made in the last year of Irving's life, when he agreed to a request by Thomas Hicks (1823–1890) to include Irving in a group portrait of America's leading intellectual and creative talents, with the writer representing the field of literature. Never without a sense of humor, Irving made the witty and oft-quoted observation that if Hicks was interested in painting his portrait, he ought hurry as, "he was dwindling away so fast, that he would soon make an excellent subject for a miniature."[18] Though the work is not known to have been realized, Hick's selection of Irving as the representative of American literature is in itself another indication of his continued status in the field, for Hicks had already painted Bryant and other major literary figures. In spite of refusing to sit or otherwise to serve as a patron of the arts, Irving nonetheless remained interested in both genre and landscape painting. Given his earlier involvement in the selection of subjects for his Anglo-American artist friends, it is hardly surprising that he took a lively interest in the various illustrated editions of his diverse writings.

The importance and popularity of those writings, both within his own lifetime and beyond, is evident in the amount of original illustration dedicated to Irving's works. His stories, histories, and biographies were interpreted by both his friends among the American artistic community and those who never had the pleasure of meeting the gracious and generous writer.

The reasons why Irving is the unsurpassed American literary source for artists are several, and some are interrelated. He was the first American writer with a national—even international—reputation, and his work and success were greeted with almost universal enthusiasm by his country's intellectual and cultural elite. His work was also singled out for praise by such highly respected and influential writers in the English language as Sir Walter Scott, Charles Dickens, and Lord Byron.[19] To be sure, boosterism colored some of the praise of Irving's work, but the quality and readability of the work, not boosterism, produced such an enduring reputation. The number of engravings, etchings, and lithographs created for both direct illustration of the later editions of Irving's books and, less often, for sale and distribution as independent pieces, reflect that popularity.

Book illustrations reached their zenith in quantity and quality during the nineteenth century, with numerous deluxe editions being printed before less expensive and lower-quality techniques of illustration and reproduction were developed. Commissioning original illustrations was not unusual in nineteenth-century publishing, but the number of well-established artists who designed illustrations for Irving's texts, in addition to those who usually made their living by that kind of work, is distinctive. Given both the large body of Irving's work and the number of editions in which his best-known pieces appeared, the quantity of illustrations is understandable, but there was no precedent for the number of famous and

*Rip Van Winkle Returning Home*, designed and etched by Felix O.C. Darley, published by *The American Art-Union*, 1848.

near-famous artists who proffered their paintings and drawings to be transferred to woodblock, engraver's plate, or lithographic stone. Leslie and Allston, fine artists with established reputations, were willing—even anxious—to supply illustrations for their good friend, as early as 1817, but they were not the first to illustrate his works. During Irving's years in Europe and prior to his second Spanish period, such renowned British illustrators as George Cruikshank (1792–1878) and Henry Sandham (1842–1912) supplied most of the designs for both the British and American editions of his works. Still later, the well-known American painters John Ehninger (1827–1889) and Frederic Church (1826–1900), among others, produced designs for the many standard and deluxe editions published by G. P. Putnam's Sons. From the late 1840s, the illustrations of Felix Octavius Carr Darley (see cat. nos. 38 and 40 and illustrations on this spread) became the best-known renditions of Irving's work and rank among the most famous book illustrations of all time. Paintings of Irving subjects were popularized in dozens of editions of prints, which again document the author's popularity.

Not only were Irving's works popular enough to warrant substantial groups of illustrations in their many editions, but the subjects were so well

*Aben Habuz, the Arabian Astrologer, and the Christian Princess*, ink drawing by Felix O.C. Darley for *The Alhambra*, New York: G.P. Putnam, 1851.

known that they inspired hundreds of independent full-scale paintings by a wide variety of American painters. John Quidor (1801–1881) devoted most of his life work to at least fifty paintings based on most of the best-known Irving subjects (cat. no. 32). Albertus D.O. Browere (1814–1887), a student of Quidor, followed the example of his teacher and painted about a dozen canvases covering many of the same themes that the older man had exhibited at the National Academy of Design and elsewhere: the popular subjects of Rip Van Winkle, The Legend of Sleepy Hollow, and various scenes based on *Diedrich Knickerbocker's A History of New-York*.[20] Other painters who completed more than one or two works taken from Irving subjects include the great Hudson Valley landscape painter, Asher B. Durand (1796–1886); the portraitist and genre painter, Henry Inman; the German-American history painter, Emanuel Leutze; and another student of Quidor, the highly successful portraitist, Charles L. Elliott. Many other American painters, artists of diverse background and training, took on at least one Irving subject during their careers—and not always at the start of their bid for professional acceptance. Included in that latter category are the founder of the American landscape school, Thomas Cole (1801–1848); the portraitist

*Spanish Dancers*, ink drawing by Felix O.C. Darley
for *The Alhambra*, New York: G.P. Putnam, 1851.

and Indian painter, Charles B. King (1785–1868); Samuel F.B. Morse (1791–1872); and the genre painter who depicted the American frontier, Tomkins Matteson (1813–1884). Even long after Irving's death, many painters including John Blair (active c. 1875) and the landscapist Ralph Blakelock (1847–1919) exhibited paintings with the subject of Rip Van Winkle.[21] Even Irving's home, Sunnyside, attracted the attention of artists (see cat. nos. 49, 51–53, 55) including George Inness, a painter not known to be a friend of Irving, who must have chosen it as a picturesque subject (cat. no. 43).

As previously noted, Irving ceased to have deep personal relationships with artists during the final American period of his life. Although his residence in Tarrytown brought him less frequently into contact with the New York art world, his reputation as an experienced connoisseur and one interested in both historical and contemporary art created many opportunities for his continued involvement with the visual arts. In addition to writing biographical entries for Dunlap's book, Irving responded to written requests for his opinion of individual works of art. Gouverneur Kemble (1786–1875), a respected industrialist and patron of the arts, asked Irving's opinion of a Durand landscape that he contemplated purchasing, and Irving responded with as specific a set of comments as one would expect from a professional critic:

It is beautiful—beautiful. Such truth of detail with such breadth; such atmosphere, such harmony, such repose, such coloring. The group of trees in the foreground is admirable; the characters of the trees so diversified and accurate; the texture and coloring of their barks; the peculiarities of their foliage. The whole picture had the effect upon me of a delightful piece of music.[22]

Nor was this reaction to landscape unique in the last few years of his life, when he strayed less often from his beloved Tarrytown. Less than a year before his death he showed his continuing appreciation of landscape painting by visiting New York to view *Heart of the Andes* by the promising young student of Thomas Cole, Frederic Church. The younger man was to show his respect in turn, providing drawings for illustrations of stories in *Crayon Miscellany* and *Tales of a Traveller* in the deluxe "New Sunnyside Edition" of Irving's collected works.

The height of Irving's reputation coincided with both the golden age of American illustration and great interest among artists in narrative painting. As Irving's reputation became more centered on the famous short stories in *The Sketch-Book*, few new artists, either in paintings or the graphic arts, attempted to challenge the established imagery associated with these works. Thus, readers in the late twentieth century still picture the heroes and scenes of Irving's most enduring writing with the images that were created nearly a century ago at the peak of his reputation.

Despite periodic changes in taste and fluctuations of the writer's reputation, Irving remains one of the most important early writers in America and a literary figure instrumental in developing taste and appreciation for the arts in the early years of the republic. Both his writings and his impact on American and Anglo-American artists form an important part of our cultural heritage.

**1.** Although most of the standard biographies of Irving at least mention all of these aspects of complicated life, only Philip McFarland (1979) attempts to put his relationships with such figures as Aaron Burr, Walter Scott, and others in a broader cultural context.

**2.** The use of the title *The Sketch-Book* itself suggests his affinity with the visual arts, but the pseudonym Geoffrey Crayon leaves no doubt as to Irving's interests. See Bowden 1981.

**3.** Many scholars have at least touched on the relationship between Irving and various artists, often in the context of a larger group (see Callow 1967), though none have so pointedly directed their study as Prown, in his unpublished, 1956 M.A. thesis, "Washington Irving's Interest in Art and His Influence Upon American Painting."

**4.** According to one of Irving's major biographers (Williams 1935: 17), one of Washington's sisters' suitors was an artist who both encouraged his interest in art and gave him a sketchbook in which to work.

**5.** Quoted in Wagenknecht 1962: 46.

**6.** From Irving's essay on Allston, New York Public Library, published in *Biographies and Other Miscellanies* and other compilations.

**7.** In a letter from Irving to Allan Cunningham, Jan. 10, 1829, New York Public Library.

**8.** Irving 1862: 1, 224.

**9.** Leslie had been much praised in Philadelphia by William Dunlap, and the latter may have introduced them. Leslie was certainly under Allston's wing since he had arrived in England, and knew of Irving and his writings long before they actually met. Newton's mother was the sister of Gilbert Stuart for whom she named her son, and she had been reared in a Tory household. Newton was reared in Boston and had traveled briefly in Italy and France before settling in England in 1817.

**10.** See Dunlap, any edition.

**11.** Prown 1956: 17.

**12.** Leslie 1860: 252, March 15, 1823.

**13.** Irving not only corresponded with artists about their mutual interests and commented on their projects both in quality and ideas but also served as their advocate whenever possible. West, Leslie, Newton, and their biographers noted this interest and enthusiasm for artists and their art.

**14.** Leslie 1860: 301.

**15.** Harvey did many sketches of Sunnyside as part of the remodelling project for which he served as artistic advisor, architect, and construction chief during Irving's many absences (see Butler 1974). He also painted the building and grounds as part of independent compositions.

**16.** Irving wrote to the Library Committee of Congress on January 7, 1847, commenting on Powell's training and artistic abilities.

**17.** For a fuller discussion of the matter of the Capitol Rotunda commissions in terms of Irving and his circle, see both Callow 1967 and Prown 1956.

**18.** As quoted in his nephew's biography of the artist, Irving 1864: 4, 300.

**19.** For a good general summation of Irving's impact, see Wagenknecht 1962: 167–169.

**20.** For fuller information on Quidor and the range and scope of his paintings based on Irving subjects, see Sokol 1973.

**21.** For the most exhaustive listing of such works, see the subject index for *Literature-Washington Irving* in the "Inventory of American Paintings" compiled in 1976 by the National Museum of American Art, Smithsonian Institution, and obtainable from the museum.

**22.** Quoted in Prown 1956: 39.

# Washington Irving:
## A CHRONOLOGY

| | |
|---|---|
| 1783 | Born in New York City on April 3. |
| 1802 | After secondary schooling and earlier clerkships, enters law office of former Attorney General J. O. Hoffman. |
| 1802–03 | Nine essays by "Jonathan Oldstyle, Gent." appear in *Morning Chronicle*. Travels up the Hudson to the Saint Lawrence River and Montreal. |
| 1804–06 | Travels in Europe. |
| 1806 | Returns to New York on March 24; passes the state bar examination November 21. |
| 1807–08 | Contributes under pseudonym to *Salmagundi*. Attends Aaron Burr's trial for treason in Richmond. |
| 1809 | *Diedrich Knickerbocker's A History of New-York* published. Fiancée Matilda Hoffman dies. |
| 1815 | Sails to England on May 15. Family import firm in Liverpool goes bankrupt in 1818; turns to professional authorship. |
| 1819–20 | *The Sketch-Book of Geoffrey Crayon, Gent.* published. |
| 1821 | Receives honorary Master of Arts (A.M.) degree from Columbia University. |
| 1822 | *Bracebridge Hall* published. Resides in Dresden. |
| 1824 | *Tales of a Traveller* published. |
| 1826 | Moves from Paris and Bordeaux to Madrid at invitation of the United States Minister to Spain. |
| 1828–1829 | Resides in Granada in apartments at the Alhambra Palace. |
| 1828 | *Life and Voyages of Christopher Columbus* published. Elected to membership in Spain's Real Academia de la Historia. |
| 1829 | *The Conquest of Granada* published. Moves to London to serve as secretary of the American Legation. Receives an honorary Doctor of Laws (LL.D.) degree from Columbia University. |

| 1830 | Receives Gold Medal in History from Royal Society of Literature, London. |
|---|---|
| 1831 | *Voyages and Discoveries of the Companions to Columbus* published. Receives an honorary Doctor in Civil Law (D.C.L.) degree from Oxford University. |
| 1831 | *The Alhambra* published. New York City greets his return with testimonial dinner. Receives honorary Doctor of Laws (LL.D.) degree from Harvard University. Tours the American West on horseback. |
| 1835 | *A Tour on the Prairies* published in *The Crayon Miscellany*. Purchases Sunnyside. |
| 1836 | *Astoria* published. Settles at Sunnyside. |
| 1838 | Declines President Van Buren's offer of cabinet post and Tammany Hall's nomination for Mayor of New York. |
| 1841 | Elected to honorary membership in the National Academy of Design. |
| 1842 | Appointed Minister to Spain by President Tyler. |
| 1846 | Returns to Sunnyside. |
| 1848 | Publication begins by G.P. Putnam of the Author's Revised Edition, to be completed in 15 volumes in 1851. |
| 1849 | Elected President of the first Board of Trustees of the Astor Library on February 14. *A Book of the Hudson* published. Elected to honorary membership in the Smithsonian Institution. |
| 1855 | *Wolfert's Roost* published, also Volume I of the *Life of George Washington*, to be followed by Volumes II and III (1856), Volume IV (1857), and Volume V (1859). |
| 1859 | Dies at Sunnyside on November 28. Service at Christ Church. Burial in Sleepy Hollow Cemetery, Tarrytown. |

# Color Plates

*Portrait of Washington Irving,* by John Wesley Jarvis, cat. no. 1.

*A Morning Rainbow, A Composition on the Grounds of R. Donaldson, Esq.*, by George Harvey, cat. no. 11.

*Lewis Gaylord Clark*, by Charles Loring Elliott, cat. no. 14.

*Self-portrait*, by Charles Robert Leslie, cat. no. 17.

*Mary Philipse*, attributed to John Wollaston, cat. no. 28.

*Washington Irving*, attributed to Charles Robert Leslie, cat. no. 18.

*George Washington*, attributed to James Sharples, Sr., cat. no. 22.

*Ichabod Crane at a Ball at Van Tassel's Mansion*, by John Quidor, cat. no. 32.

*Ichabod Crane and Katrina Van Tassel*, by Daniel Huntington, cat. no. 34.

*Joseph Jefferson as* "*Rip Van Winkle,*" by George Waters, cat. no. 37.

Drawing for "Rip Van Winkle," by Felix O.C. Darley, cat. no. 38.

Drawing for "Rip Van Winkle," by Felix O.C. Darley, cat. no. 38.

*Columbus at the Court of Ferdinand and Isabella*, by Abraham Woodside, cat. no. 41.

*Sunnyside*, by George Inness, cat. no. 43.

*Scudding Clouds After A Shower/Residence of Washington Irving Esqr.*, by George Harvey, cat. no. 46.

*Washington Irving and His Little Dog*, by Felix O.C. Darley, cat. no. 48.

*"Sunnyside," Washington Irving's House on the Hudson*, by Felix O.C. Darley, cat. no. 49.

*Sunnyside from the Hudson*, by an unknown artist, cat. no. 52.

*Sunnyside with Picnickers*, by John Henry Hill, cat. no. 55.

# Catalog

# *I* *Hudson River Landscapes*

*"How delicious it is to loll in the shade of the trees
I have planted and feel the sweet southern breeze
stealing up the green banks, and look out with half
dreaming eyes on the beautiful scenery of the Hudson
and build castles in the clouds, as I used to do,
hereabouts, in my boyhood."[1]*

So wrote Washington Irving to a favorite niece from Sunnyside in 1852. Irving is considered one of the "Kindred Spirits," a circle of artists and writers who drew direct inspiration from the scenic splendor of the Hudson River Valley and the Catskill Mountains. Irving, William Cullen Bryant, Thomas Cole, and other literary and artistic lions brought the Hudson River Valley to prominence through their popular writings and the development of the Hudson River School of painting.

The importance of place is a common theme throughout Irving's oeuvre, seen in "The Legend of Sleepy Hollow," "Rip Van Winkle," and other stories. The Manhattanite wrote about the valley long before residing there permanently. His love of the region was fostered by several trips taken up the river during his youth. Irving did not call the Hudson River Valley home for any extended period of time until 1846.

1. Letter to Sarah Paris Storrow, July 15, 1852, Historic Hudson Valley Library.

1. *Portrait of Washington Irving*
(1783–1859)

John Wesley Jarvis (1780–1840)
New York City, 1809
Oil on wood panel
33 x 26″
83.8 x 66.0 cm
SS.62.2

The Jarvis portrait is one of the best-known images of the writer, seen here as a Byronic figure on the brink of literary success. Depicted in a romantic mode with tousled hair and fur-collared wrap, the sitter is posed with body facing left and head turned in a three-quarter view.

N. P. Willis noted the presence of the portrait at Sunnyside, Irving's home, in the November 19, 1859, issue of the *Home Journal*, and all available documentation suggests that the portrait has hung there ever since.[1]

Jarvis captured this evocative image in 1809, a watershed year for the young writer. Irving's first highly popular offering, *Diedrich Knickerbocker's A History of New-York*, was published and acclaimed, serving as the basis for his international reputation. Irving would also remember 1809 for a great personal tragedy, the death of his fiancée, Matilda Hoffman. Pierre M. Irving, the writer's nephew and biographer, wrote of the portrait:

> Although the poignancy of his grief [at the death of Matilda Hoffman] had worn away when he returned to the city, his countenance long retained the trace of melancholy feelings. A portrait of Jarvis taken some months afterwards, and conceded without dissent at that time, to be a faithful and admirable likeness, is remarkable for its expression of pensive refinement.[2]

John Wesley Jarvis, one of the greatest portrait painters working in New York during the first quarter of the nineteenth century, was born in England. As a child he emigrated to Philadelphia with his family and served as an apprentice to the engraver

Edward Savage. He moved to New York in 1802 and worked there for most of his career, excluding a few years spent in Baltimore. His apprentices included John Quidor (1801–1881) and Henry Inman (1801–1846). Jarvis was also known for his social skill as a conversationalist.[3]

Provenance: Irving family possession; Louis du Pont Irving, 1945.

Exhibition: "The American Portrait: From the Death of Stuart to the Rise of Sargent," Worcester, MA: Worcester Art Museum, 1973.

References: 1., 2. Irving 1862–1864, 1, pp. 229, 232, 261–62, 274–76; 4, p. 315; 3. Groce and Wallace 1957, p. 346; Theodore Bolton and George C. Groce, "John Wesley Jarvis, An Account of His Life and the First Catalogue of His Portraits," *Art Quarterly* 1 (Autumn 1938), pp. 299–321; Butler 1983, p. 192; Joseph T. Butler "Washington Irving, Romanticism, and Sunnyside: Part I," *Connoisseur* 167 (January 1968), pp. 51–57, illus. pl. 1; Butler 1974, pl. 1; Mary B. Cowdrey, *American Academy of Fine Arts and American Art-Union, Exhibition Record 1816–1852*, New York: New-York Historical Society, 1953, p. 207; Marshall B. Davidson, *The American Heritage History of Writer's America*, New York: American Heritage Publishing Company, 1973, p. 79; Harold E. Dickson, *John Wesley Jarvis, American Painter, 1780–1840, with a checklist of his works*, New York: New-York Historical Society, 1949, no. 108; William J. Hennessey, *The American Portrait: From the Death of Stuart to the Rise of Sargent*, Worcester, MA: Worcester Art Museum, 1973, no. 4; Kenneth S. Lynn, "Washington Irving Saw the Past—Sunnyside Up," *Smithsonian* 14:5 (August 1983), pp. 92–102; Myers 1972, illus. on cover; Knoedler 1946, frontispiece.
KEJ

## 2. *Novi Belgii in America Septentrionali*

Matthew Seutter (1678–1757), engraver
Germany, 1730–1740
Hand-colored engraving
19½ x 22½"
49.5 x 57.2 cm
PM.69.1

Incorporating an area from the Saint Lawrence River to the north and Virginia to the south, the Seutter map epitomizes the mixture of reality and fantasy with which eighteenth-century Europeans viewed the New World. The not very accurate but fanciful rendering features the Hudson River in the center with Long Island or "Insula Longa" at its mouth as well as an inset cityscape of the tip of Manhattan, the so-called Restitutio View of New Amsterdam, borrowed from Nikolaus J. Visscher of the Netherlands, who had executed the original c. 1656. Irving satirized the seventeenth-century settlers of New York in *Diedrich Knickerbocker's A History of New-York* (1809), his own comic portrait of New Netherland.

Provenance: Old Print Shop, New York City, 1969.

References: E. Benézit, *Dictionnaire Critique et Documentaire des Peintres, Sculpteurs, Dessinateurs et Graveurs de tous temps et de tous les pays par un groupe d'écrivains spécialistes français et étrangers*, 10 vols., reprint, Paris: Librarie Grund, 1976, 9, p. 548; Butler 1983, p. 39; *From Lenape Territory to Royal Province, New Jersey, 1600–1750*, Trenton, NJ: New Jersey State Museum, 1971, Visscher map illus. no. 97; *The Old Print Shop Portfolio* 28 (January 1969), p. 113; I.N. Phelps Stokes, *The Iconography of Manhattan Island*, 6 vols., New York: Robert H. Dodd, 1915–1918, Restitutio View 1, pl. 8–b, Seutter map illus. 1, pl. 16–b.
KEJ

3. *View of Phillip's Manner [sic] and the Rocks on the Hudson or North River, North America*
Unknown artist "D.R."
New York, 1784
Watercolor on paper
19¼ x 26¼"
48.9 x 66.7 cm
PM.65.866
Gift of La Duchesse de Talleyrand

At the time of Irving's birth, the lower Hudson Valley was dotted with farmsteads and both saw and grist mills. In Yonkers, the Philipse family had established an agricultural and commercial complex at the confluence of the Hudson and Nepperhan rivers that endured for nearly one hundred years. During the American revolution, both this site, referred to as "Lower Mills," and the "Upper Mills" in present-day North Tarrytown, now Philipsburg Manor, were seized from the Philipse family by the New York Committee of Forfeiture because of the family's Tory stance. Executed one year after Washington Irving's birth in Manhattan, this wash drawing is a rare visual documentation of an eighteenth-century Hudson Valley farmstead and milling site that includes manor house, barn, mill, hay barracks, sheepcote, and possible warehouses.

The drawing is inscribed with the title and following on reverse: "June 18th, 1784/D.R. fecit."

Provenance: Honorable D. McN. K. Stauffer; La Duchesse de Talleyrand, New York City, 1944.

Exhibition: "Divided Loyalties," Philipsburg Manor, North Tarrytown, NY, 1976–1979.

References: Butler 1983, p. 38; Edward H. Hall, *Philipse Manor Hall at Yonkers, N.Y., the Site, the Building, and Its Occupants*, New York: The American Scenic and Historic Preservation Society, 1912, pl. 1; Keller 1976, p. 227; Hugh G. Rowell, "Philipse Castle, 1683–1944," *American Collector* 13 (May 1944), pp. 5–6.
KEJ

4. *View from West Point*
Rebecca Phoenix
New York City, January 1795
Watercolor on paper
16 x 21¼"
40.6 x 54 cm
VC.58.544

As indicated by the inscriptions found on the lower corners, "Rebecca Phoenix" and "Columbian Academy New York Jany 1795," the artist studied at the art school run by the Scottish brothers Alexander (1772–1814) and Archibald Robertson (1765–1835). Alexander Robertson executed a series of Hudson River views, including those of West Point, and Miss Phoenix probably copied one of his sketches.

Washington Irving lived near the Robertson family on William Street in Manhattan and counted them as close friends. According to an early biographer, Irving studied sketching at the academy as well.[1]

Little is known about the artist. The 1790 census lists households headed by Daniel Phoenix and Philip Phoenix in New York City.[2]

Provenance: Fred Johnson, Kingston, New York.

References: 1. Williams 1935, 1, p. 384; 2. *Heads of Families at the First Census of the United States Taken in the Year 1790, New York*, Baltimore: Genealogical Publishing, 1971, pp. 118, 127.
KEJ

3

4

## 5. *Mill at Philipsburg Manor*

William Rickarby Miller (1818–1893)
Probably New York City, 1869
Oil on canvas
17¾ x 25½"
45.1 x 64.8 cm
PM.65.862

Miller's pastoral scene of house and mill exists in several versions. The New-York Historical Society owns the original sepia drawing of 1851; Historic Hudson Valley's collection also includes a watercolor version dated 1852. A woodcut of the same scene appeared in *Gleason's Pictorial Drawing-Room Companion* the following year. According to Richard Koke, Miller often reworked sketches, sometimes decades after the original had been executed.[1]

The following notation was made by Miller more than thirty years after he drew his on-site sketch:

The sketch was made in August 1851. It included the old Beekman's Mill, and the Old Phillip's Mansion surrounded by its old trees—the whole scene is close to the Old Dutch Church in Sleepy Hollow, Beekmantown, N.Y., where Washington Irving lies burried [sic]. The old "Ichabod Crane" bridge was close to where I sat. (July 1885)[2]

A landscape painter and commercial artist, Miller produced hundreds of watercolors and oils, many of which were engraved and reproduced in books and periodicals. Born in England, Miller had emigrated to New York City during the winter of 1844–1845 and spent most of his career in and around this city. After 1873 he devoted himself to producing pen-and-ink sketches for a planned but never-published project, "One Hundred Gems" of American landscape.[3]

Provenance: 1943.

Exhibitions: "Time, Man and the River," Hudson River Museum, Yonkers, NY, 1977.

References: 1. Personal correspondence, Richard J. Koke, Curator, New-York Historical Society, to Joseph T. Butler, Curator, Sleepy Hollow Restorations, December 13, 1976; 2. Koke 1982, 2, pp. 350–351; 3. Groce and Wallace 1957, p. 446; Butler 1983, p. 36; Grace M. Carlock, "William Rickarby Miller (1818–1893)," *New-York Historical Society Quarterly* 31 (October 1947), pp. 199–209, watercolor version illustrated; *Gleason's Pictorial Drawing-Room Companion* 5 (November 26, 1853), woodcut version illus.; Hugh G. Rowell, "Philipse Castle, 1683–1944," *American Collector* 13 (May 1944), pp. 5–6.
KEJ

## 6. *Panorama of Philipsburg Manor, Upper Mills, and Old Dutch Church*

Unknown artist
America, mid-nineteenth century
Oil on canvas
27 x 34"
68.6 x 86.4 cm
PM.71.4

By taking license with perspective, an unknown artist working in a folk style has captured all of "Sleepy Hollow," an area made famous by Irving in one of the stories published in *The Sketch-Book of Geoffrey Crayon, Gent.* (1819). Natural and man-made features include (from left to right): a bridge crossing the Pocantico River, the confluence of the Pocantico and Hudson rivers, a mill and manor house, the Old Dutch Church and surrounding cemetery, and the "Headless Horseman Bridge," which Ichabod Crane strove to reach in order to escape the phantom rider.

Oval stencil on reverse of canvas reads: "Williams, Stevens & Williams/ Looking Glass House/Art Repository/ Engravings, Art Materials, etc./353 Broadway, N.Y."

Provenance: Kipper (unknown vendor), 1945.
KEJ

5

6

## 7. *Old Dutch Church at Sleepy Hollow*

William Rickarby Miller (1818–1893)
Probably New York, 1861
Oil on canvas
14 x 21½"
34.6 x 56.6 cm
SS.79.3
Gift of Mr. and Mrs. E.W. Harden

Built in 1699 by Frederick Philipse, the first Lord of Philipsburg Manor, and his second wife, Catherine Van Cortlandt Philipse, the Dutch Reformed (Old Dutch) Church was immortalized in Irving's "The Legend of Sleepy Hollow." The church today maintains an appearance similar to that depicted in the Miller painting, including renovations made to the exterior and interior during the 1840s. The classical portico, which was also added in the 1840s, fell into disrepair and was removed decades later.

William Rickarby Miller is responsible for at least three versions of this scene. This oil on canvas and a watercolor rendering, which bears the date August 11, 1851, are in the collection of Historic Hudson Valley. A woodcut version, which appeared in an 1853 issue of *Gleason's Pictorial Drawing-Room Companion*, was the first of many illustrations that Miller executed for weekly newspapers.[1]

The painting is signed and dated in the lower right: "W.R. Miller/1861."

Provenance: Mr. and Mrs. E. W. Harden, 1948.

Exhibition: "Washington Irving," Grolier Club, New York City, 1983.

References: 1. Grace Miller Carlock, "William Rickarby Miller (1818–1893)," *The New-York Historical Society Quarterly* 31:4 (October 1947), pp. 199–212; *Gleason's Pictorial Drawing-Room Companion* 4:20 (January 8, 1853), p. 1.
KEJ

## 8. *The Capture of Major Andre*

Unknown artist
United States, mid-nineteenth century (post 1834)
Oil on canvas
22½ x 29"
57.2 x 73.7 cm
SS.82.2
Bequest of Mrs. Alexander Duer Irving

"Sleepy Hollow" not only served as the fictional setting for Irving's tale but is remembered as the actual locale where Major John Andre was captured during the Revolutionary War. Andre, an Adjutant General in the British Army and an aide to Sir Henry Clinton, entered into a plot with the traitorous Patriot General Benedict Arnold to secure plans and details of fortifications under Arnold's command, including those of West Point. After meeting with Arnold aboard the British vessel *The Vulture* off Teller's Point (near present-day Croton) and receiving the secret documents, Andre headed south on the Albany Post Road, dressed in civilian clothing, with the compromising papers tucked into his boots. Three Patriot farm boys, John Paulding, Issac Van Wart, and David Williams, apprehended Andre in the Tarrytown area on September 23, 1780. He was hung as a spy ten days later.

An engraving published by the American Art-Union in 1845, based on Asher B. Durand's original painting of 1834, may well have served as a design source for this less-skilled version.

Provenance: Mrs. Alexander Duer Irving, Wilmington, DE, 1982.

References: *A. B. Durand 1796–1886*, Montclair, NJ: Montclair Art Museum, 1971, no. 28; Maybelle Mann, *The American Art-Union*, Otisville, NY: ALM Associates, 1977, p. 45.
KEJ

7

8

## 9. Chairs

Probably New York, 1835–1840
Maple, ash
33¾ x 18 x 20″
85.6 x 45.7 x 50.8 cm
SS.89.15 and SS.89.20
Gift of Miss Isabel Scriba

These two painted chairs, from a set of eight, were once owned by the Cruger family in Montrose, New York. According to family tradition, the landscapes painted on the back supports depict Hudson River Valley scenes, although no feature can be specifically associated with the locale. The scenes combine stencilled and freehand decoration rendered in metallic powders. Similar landscape decoration appears on window valance boards with a Westchester County history.[1]

Provenance: Dr. Gouverneur Cruger; Miss Isabel Scriba, Garden City, NY, 1989.

Exhibition: "American Painted Furniture, 1800 to World War I," Scarsdale Historical Society, Scarsdale, NY, 1990.

References: 1. James Archer Abbott and Joseph T. Butler, *American Painted Furniture, 1800 to World War I*, Scarsdale, NY: Scarsdale Historical Society, 1990, nos. 6–7; Dean A. Fales, Jr., *American Painted Furniture, 1660–1880*, New York: E.P. Dutton, 1972, pp. 188–189.
KEJ

**10.** *Early Twilight, Kaatskill Landing and Mountains from the East Bank of the Hudson River, N.Y.*

George Harvey (1800/01–1878)
New York, 1830–1840
Watercolor and gouache on paper
10 x 14¾"
25.4 x 37.5 cm
SS.79.37
Bequest of Mrs. Frederick Lydecker

Although relatively little is known about him, George Harvey figures as one of the more intriguing "Kindred Spirits." Emigrating to the United States in 1820, this English-born artist spent several years in the western wilderness hunting, composing prose and poetry, and sketching. Based on his early work, he was elected to the National Academy of Design in 1828. In a completely different vein, he then established a career as a miniaturist in Boston, earning a reputation for his prolific output. His success took a toll on his health and forced him to retire from this line of employment. In 1836 he purchased land in Hastings, New York, and created an Elizabethan-style cottage nestled in a romantic landscape. Concurrently, Harvey oversaw the renovations of Sunnyside, a former tenant farmhouse on Philipsburg Manor that his friend Irving had recently purchased. Harvey's talents were myriad.[1]

A forerunner of the Luminist Movement, Harvey was interested in capturing the effect of atmospheric conditions on landscape. He executed a series of watercolored "Atmospheric Views," which he hoped would be reproduced as engravings, but *Harvey's Scenes in the Primeval Forests of America, at the Four Periods of the Year* (1841), consisting of four engravings, was the only resulting publication. In hopes of garnering financial support for the project, Harvey formed a touring exhibition of watercolors. A gallery guide to the exhibition survives, as do many of the works included in it.

*Early Twilight* was one of the scenes Harvey exhibited, but it is unclear if this was the landscape now owned by Historic Hudson Valley or a nearly identical version in the collection of the New-York Historical Society. The hand-lettered mat on the New-York Historical Society's version is similar to those found on other watercolors displayed by Harvey and probably was executed with public exhibition in mind. Historic Hudson Valley's version has also been titled *View from Osborne's Hilltop* because of a pencilled inscription on the back of the watercolor. It is signed "G. Harvey" in the lower left corner.

Little is known of Harvey's career after 1850. It seems likely that he returned to England, although he is also known to have made painting expeditions to Newport, Rhode Island, Florida, and Bermuda.

Provenance: Mrs. Frederick Lydecker

Exhibitions: "Drawings of the Hudson River School," The Brooklyn Museum, Brooklyn, NY, 1969; "The Catskills: Painters, Writers, and Tourists in the Mountains 1820–1895," Hudson River Museum of Westchester, Yonkers, NY, 1988–1989.

References: 1. Groce and Wallace 1957, p. 298; Harvey 1850, no. 33; Koke 1982, 2, no. 1156; Jo Miller, *Drawings of the Hudson River School*, Brooklyn, NY: The Brooklyn Museum, 1969, fig. 71; Kenneth Myers, *The Catskills: Painters, Writers, and Tourists in the Mountains 1820–1895*, Yonkers, NY: Hudson River Museum of Westchester, 1987, pl. 86; Donald A. Shelley, "George Harvey, English Painter of Atmospheric Landscapes in America," *American Collector* 17 (April 1948), pp. 10–13.
KEJ

11. *A Morning Rainbow,*
*A Composition on the Grounds of*
*R. Donaldson, Esq.*

George Harvey (c. 1800/01–1878)
New York, 1840–1850
Watercolor on paper
9¾ x 13⅞″
24.8 x 35.2 cm
SS.63.24

The view from this estate in clear weather is very extensive, showing the lofty range of the Catskill Mountains in the West. The continually increasing amount of merchandise freighted up and down the magnificent Hudson river makes the scene, in summer, very animated....A morning rainbow is of such unusual occurrence that Mr. Harvey has seen but two; the first one seemed to him so singular and picturesque that he made a memorandum sketch, which he has adapted to the present scene.

The artist having repeatedly experienced a most courteous hospitality from the refined and accomplished family resident at Blythwood...The morning rainbow, therefore, he has introduced into the drawing, as referring to a moral fact rather than to the physical occurrence of the phenomenon. His days of sojourn with them were so sunny that no cloud obscured the landscape, nor cast its shadows on his mental prospect.[1]

Robert Donaldson's estate, Blithewood, situated in present-day Annandale-on-Hudson, New York, served as an icon of American Romanticism as expressed through landscape and architectural design. Andrew Jackson Downing (1815–1852) dedicated *Cottage Residences* (1844) to "Robert Donaldson, Esq. of Blithewood, on the Hudson"[2] and the house was later employed as the frontispiece of his 1849 edition of *A Treatise on the Theory and Practice of Landscape Gardening*. He visited there with Swedish novelist Fredrika Bremer who recorded her reminiscences of "that sublime and glorious landscape."[3]

For biographical information on George Harvey, see entry no. 10.

Provenance: Kennedy Galleries, New York City, 1946.

References: 1. Harvey 1850, pp. 16–17; 2. A. J. Downing, *A Treatise on the Theory and Practice of Landscape Gardening, Adapted to American with a View to the Improvement of Country Residences...with Remarks on Rural Architecture*, seventh edition, New York: Orange Judd Agricultural Book Publisher, 1865, pp. 30–31, illus. as frontispiece; 3. Frederika Bremer, *The Homes of the New World, Impressions of America*, 2 vols., New York: Harper & Brothers, 1856, 1, pp. 33–37; Butler 1983, p. 214; Groce and Wallace 1957, p. 298; George Harvey, *Harvey's Illustrations of the forest wilds & uncultivated wastes of Our Country*, Boston: Dutton & Wentworth, 1851, p. 33; Donald A. Shelley, "George Harvey, English Painter of Atmospheric Landscapes in America," *American Collector* 17 (April 1948), pp. 10–13.
KEJ

# *II* *Irving and his Circle*

WASHINGTON IRVING'S INTER-ests were never limited to litera-ture. Although the writer claimed to be neither artist nor politician, he proved quite successful at both. Early in his life, while touring Rome with his friend Washington Allston, Irving asked: "Why might not I remain here and turn painter?"[1] The author's letters and journals often included detailed sketches of people and places he visited. His twenty-four-year expansion of his country cottage, Sunnyside, also attests to his artistic as well as architectural skill. Martin Van Buren and Daniel Webster were among those who recognized his social and political observations as astute and often correct. Irving was, indeed, a man of many talents.

Because of his diverse interests, Irving's circle of friends included painters, actors, politicians, as well as writers. He was one of those rare people who could befriend both sides of an argument. And, because of his popularity as one of America's first great writers, he was often in a position to offer assistance and advice to others, no matter what their field of interest.

1. Knoedler 1946, p. 27.

## 12. *Washington Irving and His Literary Friends at Sunnyside*

Christian Schussele (1824/26?–1879)
Philadelphia, 1863
Oil on canvas
50⅜ x 75⅝″
128.0 x 192.1 cm
SS.79.47
Gift of John D. Rockefeller, Jr.

Irving was a central figure in the formation and development of a distinctly American body of literature. Artist Christian Schussele attempted to convey that concept through this canvas, which was based on a Felix O.C. Darley steel engraving that was published in London in 1863. Here, in an aggrandized view of the late author's study at Sunnyside, fourteen of Irving's fellow

writers are depicted, left to right: Henry T. Tuckerman (1813–1871), Oliver Wendell Holmes (1809–1894), William Gilmore Simms (1806–1870), Fitz-Greene Halleck (1790–1867), Nathaniel Hawthorne (1804–1864), Henry Wadsworth Longfellow (1807–1882), Nathaniel Parker Willis (1806–1867), William H. Prescott (1796–1859), Irving, James Kirke Paulding (1778–1860), Ralph Waldo Emerson (1803–1882), William Cullen Bryant (1794–1878), John Pendleton Kennedy (1795–1870), James Fenimore Cooper (1789–1851), and George Bancroft (1800–1891). A gathering of these men never took place—indeed, Cooper, Paulding, Prescott, and Irving were already deceased when the picture was painted. But many of these

men had visited Irving at Sunnyside. Cooper and Bryant were indebted to Irving for assistance in obtaining publishers for foreign editions of their works; Paulding and Kennedy were not only fellow writers but longtime friends and confidants of Irving. Others in the painting saw Irving not as a personal acquaintance but as a mentor who had paved the way for their own literary success.

Christian Schussele was born in the French province of Alsace. He studied painting in Strasbourg and Paris and emigrated to the United States in 1848. Settling in Philadelphia, Schussele painted portraits, landscapes, and historical and genre scenes. This painting, signed in the left corner, "C. Schussele/1863," was completed at about the time the artist was affected with palsy. Although his skill and precision were greatly altered by the disease, Schussele continued to paint until his death in 1879.[1]

The National Portrait Gallery owns a nearly identical version painted by Schussele.

Provenance: A. T. Stewart, New York City, 1887; John Perry, Tarrytown, NY, 1953; John D. Rockefeller, Jr., New York City, 1953.

Exhibitions: "Washington Irving and His Circle," M. Knoedler and Company, New York City, 1946; "This New Man: A Discourse in Portraits," National Portrait Gallery, Washington, DC, 1968.

References: 1. Frances M. Wilson, "'Washington Irving and His Literary Friends at Sunnyside,' Christian Schusselle, Artist," unpublished paper, Washington DC, 1973; Butler 1983, p. 206; ...illustrated by Darley 1978, no. 99; Faison and Mills 1982, p. 19; *America Through the Eyes of German Immigrant Painters*, Boston: Goethe Institute, 1975, p. 41; Knoedler 1946, no. 60; *Sketches of Distinguished American Authors represented in Darley's New National Picture, entitled Washington Irving and His Literary Friends at Sunnyside*, New York: Irving Publishing Company, 1863; *Catalog of the A. T. Stewart Collection of paintings, sculptures and other objects of art*, New York: American Art Association, 1887, no. 57.
JAA

## 13. *James Fenimore Cooper* (1789–1851)

Charles Loring Elliott (1812–1868)
Probably New York City, 1835–1851
Oil on canvas
18 x 14″
45.7 x 35.6 cm
SS.79.46

James Fenimore Cooper has been described as an influential yet controversial figure in mid-nineteenth-century literary circles. Such works as *The Pilot* (1823), *The Last of the Mohicans* (1826), and *The Bravo* (1831) serve as testament to Cooper's role in the development of American literature and its appreciation abroad. His expressions of discontent with the American way of life in the late 1830s, however, resulted in the loss of popularity that he never regained in his lifetime.

Cooper's first successful work, *The Spy*, which was published in 1821, quickly became the largest-selling American work of that time. Irving advised Cooper on possible publishing sources for a European edition of this work. Irving considered himself one of Cooper's many admirers: "I have a great desire to make his acquaintance," he wrote after missing meeting Cooper during their respective 1827 visits to Paris. "I am delighted with his novels."[1]

Irving and Cooper did eventually meet. But their subsequent friendship often fell victim to Cooper's jealousy of the critical acclaim afforded Irving. In memoriam to Cooper, Irving wrote: "In life they judge a writer by his last production; after death by what he has done best.... So it will be with Cooper."[2] Irving believed Cooper's later works criticizing his fellow countrymen would be overshadowed by the significance of his work as a whole. This has proven true.

Charles Loring Elliott studied with both John Trumbull (1756–1843) and John Quidor (1801–1881). A popular artist, Elliott concentrated on portraiture. Among the more than 700 portraits known to have been painted by him are notable images of poet Fitz-Greene Halleck, railroad executive Erastus Corning, and brewer and college founder Matthew Vassar.

Provenance: Jane Cooper Bland; M. Knoedler and Company, New York City, 1949.

Exhibitions: "Washington Irving and His Circle," M. Knoedler and Company, New York City, 1946; "The Catskills: Painters, Writers, and Tourists in the Mountains 1820–1895," Hudson River Museum of Westchester, Yonkers, NY, 1988–1989.

References: 1., 2. Aderman et al. 1979, 2, pp. 225–228; Theodore Bolton, "Charles Loring Elliott: An Account of His Life and Work" and "A Catalogue of the Portraits Painted by Charles Loring Elliott," *Art Quarterly* 5 (Winter 1942), pp. 59–96, no. 23; Butler 1983, p. 197; Groce and Wallace 1957, p. 210; Kenneth Myers, *The Catskills: Painters, Writers, and Tourists in the Mountains 1820–1895*, Yonkers, NY: Hudson River Museum of Westchester, 1987, p. 87.
JAA

## 14. *Lewis Gaylord Clark*
(1808–1873)

Charles Loring Elliott (1812–1868)
New York, c. 1846
Oil on canvas
20½ x 17½″
52.0 x 44.4 cm
SS.79.45

Lewis Gaylord Clark ranked as one of the most influential figures in mid-nineteenth-century New York. As editor and part owner of the *Knicker-bocker Magazine*, Clark sought articles and essays from friends like Irving, William Cullen Bryant, and Henry Wadsworth Longfellow. Irving found the obligation of writing for the magazine sometimes "irksome," however, continuing that "the proprietors of the magazine...are not punctual in their pay."[1]

Clark, one of the founders of New York's prestigious Century Association, was an intimate of Irving. Some of their shared experiences served as enjoyable reading in Clark's own column, "Gossip with Readers and Correspondents." One amusing episode included in Clark's column occurred during a thunderstorm. While Irving sought shelter under a tree, Clark remained out in the pouring rain. He excused himself by explaining that once his father had sought shelter under a chestnut tree during a thunderstorm. The tree was struck by lightning, and Clark's father remained unconscious for several hours. Recovered, the father told his son never to stand under a tree during a thunderstorm. "Oh!" said Irving, "that makes all the difference in the world. If it is hereditary, and lightning runs in your family, you are wise."[2]

Exhibitions: National Academy of Design, New York, 1846, number 215; "Washington Irving and His Circle," M. Knoedler Galleries, New York City, 1946.

References: 1. Aderman et al. 1982, 3, pp. 71–73; 2. Knoedler 1946, pp. 46–47.
JAA

## 15. *William Cullen Bryant*
(1794–1878)

Attributed to Asher B. Durand
(1796–1886)
United States, 1854
Oil on canvas
29¼ x 24½″
74.3 x 62.2 cm
SS.79.36

William Cullen Bryant was one of this country's first great poets. A lawyer and journalist, Bryant was also well known for his vocal support of such sensitive mid-nineteenth-century issues as free trade and antislavery; his published opinions are said to have influenced Abraham Lincoln's issuance of the Emancipation Proclamation.

Bryant's relationship with Irving, however, was based not on politics but on a mutual appreciation of this country's natural beauty. In 1831 Bryant asked Irving for assistance in finding a publisher for a London edition of his collected poems. The poems were eventually published, in part because Irving agreed to edit them and write an accompanying dedication. Of Bryant's poems, Irving wrote "they transport us into the depths of the solemn forest, to the shores of the lonely lake, the banks of the wild, nameless stream, or the brow of the rocky upland, rising like a promontory from amidst a wide ocean of foliage."[1] For Irving, Bryant's words described all that was beautiful in their "youthful,...free,...rising country."

The son of a watchmaker, Asher Brown Durand worked as an engraver before developing an interest in painting. Considered, along with Thomas Cole, one of the founders of the Hudson River School of painting, Durand sought to illustrate visually the romantic beauty of the landscape that Bryant, Irving, and others so often described in their writings. A charter member of the National Academy of Design, Durand served as the organization's president from 1845 to 1861.

Provenance: Mrs. William Cullen Bryant; New York Public Library; M. Knoedler and Company, New York City, 1949.

Exhibitions: "Washington Irving and His Circle," M. Knoedler and Company, New York City, 1946; Executive Mansion, Albany, NY, 1961–1975; "A. B. Durand, 1796–1886," Montclair Art Museum, Montclair, NJ, 1971; "Hudson Valley People, Albany to Yonkers, 1700–1900," Vassar College Art Gallery, Poughkeepsie, NY, 1982.

References: 1. Knoedler 1946, illus. 30; Butler 1983, p. 203; *A. B. Durand, 1796–1886*, Montclair, NJ: Montclair Art Museum, 1971, fig. 71; Faison and Mills 1982, p. 47; David B. Lawall, *Asher B. Durand, His Art and Art Theory in Relation to His Times*, New York: Garland Publishing, 1977, fig. 50; *Who Was Who in America: 1607–1896*, Chicago: A.N. Marquis, 1967, p. 150.
JAA

14

15

**16. *Sir Walter Scott* (1771–1832)**

Gilbert Stuart Newton (1794–1835)
England, c. 1826
Pastel and pencil on paper
5½ x 5″
14.0 x 12.7 cm
SS.79.41

Sir Walter Scott, Scottish poet, historian, biographer, and novelist, was both a friend and mentor of Irving. The young American had admired Scott's writing for many years prior to their introduction in 1817. In that year, while Irving was traveling through Scotland, he called upon Scott at his home, Abbotsford, where he was welcomed into the family and invited to join Scott on walks through the countryside. It has often been suggested that Scott's writings dealing with local folklore and history were an inspiration for Irving's own American tales. Certainly Scott's romantic Abbotsford served as a model for Irving's cottage along the Hudson, Sunnyside.

Gilbert Stuart Newton was introduced to Scott by Irving in 1826. The present drawing is inscribed, "Sir Walter Scott/To Inman Esq/with the complts of/G.S. Newton." Henry Inman (1801–1846) was an American painter successful with both landscape and portrait painting.

Provenance: Henry Inman; Irving family possession; Louis du Pont Irving, 1945.

References: Butler 1983, p. 209, 226; Groce and Wallace 1957, p. 470; Andrew B. Myers, "Washington Irving and Gilbert Stuart Newton: A *New York Mirror* Contribution Identified," *Bulletin of the New York Public Library* 76 (1972), pp. 237–241; Williams 1935.
JAA

**17. *Self-portrait***

Charles Robert Leslie (1794–1859)
England, 1815–1830
Oil on canvas
24½ x 19¾″
62.2 x 50.2 cm
SS.80.2

Charles Robert Leslie was born in London of American parents. He studied painting with both Benjamin West (1738–1820) and Washington Allston (1779–1843) and, beginning in 1813, exhibited at the Royal Academy of Art. Between 1828 and 1854, Leslie exhibited works at the National Academy of Design in New York City. He also taught drawing for a brief time at the United States Military Academy at West Point.[1]

As his art training might suggest, Leslie considered England to be his permanent home. It was in London that the artist first met Irving. In 1820 the two men toured England together, forming the foundation for what would become a lifelong friendship. "I not only owe you some of the happiest social hours of my life," wrote Leslie to Irving, "but you opened to me a new range of observation in my art, and a perception of qualities and characters of things which painters do not always imbibe from each other."[2] It was through Leslie that Irving became acquainted with other artists, among them fellow American Gilbert Stuart Newton. Irving, Leslie, and Newton were seen as a trio of talent, influencing one another's work. James Thomas Flexner noted that when Irving "was writing his *Sketch-Book*, he saw every step they [Leslie and Newton] made on their art, and they saw every line of writing."[3]

This self-portrait is inscribed on the back, "To Eliza. C.R. Leslie Pinx." The portrait was painted for Leslie's sister, Eliza.

Provenance: Eliza Leslie, Gertrude Leslie, Lakehurst, NJ; Hiram Burlington, New York City; Chester Dale, New York City; M. Knoedler and Company, New York City, 1946.

Exhibitions: "American Paintings from the Chester Dale Collection," Union League Club, New York City, 1937; "Washington Irving and His Circle," M. Knoedler and Company, New York City, 1946; "Return to Albion, Americans in England 1760–1940," National Portrait Gallery, Washington, DC, 1979.

References: 1. Groce and Wallace 1957, p. 394; 2. Knoedler 1946, no. 18; 3. Myers 1976, pp. 415–417; Butler 1983, p. 193; Richard Kenin, *Return to Albion, Americans in England, 1760–1940*, Washington, DC: National Portrait Gallery, 1979, no. 59; Richard Kenin, *Return to Albion, Americans in England 1760–1940*, New York: Holt, Rinehart and Winston, 1979, p. 68; *Who Was Who in America: 1607–1896*, Chicago: A.N. Marquis, 1967, p. 382.
JAA

16

17

18. *Washington Irving* (1783–1859)
Attributed to Charles Robert Leslie
(1794–1859)
England, c. 1820
Oil on canvas
9⅞ x 8⅛"
24.8 x 20.3 cm
SS.87.6
Bequest of Miss Joan Augusta Van Wart

In 1820 Irving was again in Europe, no longer as the exploring tourist but as the popular young American writer. His *Sketch-Book* proved a great success with English readers, even though originally he had difficulties in securing a publisher for the work. With this new-found fame, Irving became a popular figure in social circles. His portrait by his friend Charles Leslie captured Irving at this point in his life. Regarding a similar Leslie image of himself, Irving asked the painter "only [to] be careful to finish the picture so as not to give too fixed and precise a fashion of dress. I preferred the costume of Newton's likeness of me, which was trimmed with fur. These modern dresses are apt to give a paltry common placed [sic] air."[1]

Although this painting does not display the requested fur collar, the existing costume does avoid "any present fashion that might in a few years appear stupid."[2]

Provenance: Mr. Irving Van Wart, Miss Joan Augusta Van Wart, Brighton, Sussex, United Kingdom, 1987.

References: 1. Aderman et al. 1978, 1, pp. 603–605; 2. Aderman et al 1978, 1, pp. 610–612.
JAA

19. *Washington Irving* (1783–1859)
John Vanderlyn (1776–1852)
Paris, France, 1805
Pencil on artist's board
9½ x 7³⁄₁₆"
24.13 x 18.2 cm
SS.87.5
Bequest of Miss Joan Augusta Van Wart

Like many of his contemporaries, Irving toured Europe as a further stage in his education. In 1805, during his grand tour, Irving met a young New York artist named John Vanderlyn who had been sent to Europe by the New York Academy of the Fine Arts to purchase plaster casts of ancient sculptures for its collection. The two became close friends, as the following excerpts from Irving's diary of June 1805 suggest:

> 4th—Left Hotel Richelieu and took room the other side of the Seine— in the neighborhood of Vanderlyn.
> 6th—Dined with Vanderlyn at a Swiss restaurateur's in Louvre— cheap...
> 8th—Went with Vanderlyn to theatre of Port St. Martin...
> 13th—Went to a 15–sous ball in Palais Royal with Vanderlyn.[1]

Vanderlyn's mission for the Academy ran into financial difficulties, leaving the artist stranded. Irving himself sought assistance for his friend through letters home. The interest of another fellow American in the artist's work led to Vanderlyn's rescue: Philadelphian William McClure gave the artist money to study in Rome for three years. In 1808 Vanderlyn exhibited at the Paris Salon, winning the gold medal award. He returned to the United States in 1815, eventually becoming one of the country's premier portrait artists.

This half-length portrait of Irving seated in an upholstered armchair was presumably drawn by Vanderlyn in Paris in the summer of 1805. It, or a more finished version of this drawing, inspired several popular engravings produced throughout the nineteenth century.

Provenance: Mr. Irving Van Wart; Miss Joan Augusta Van Wart, Brighton, Sussex, United Kingdom, 1987.

References: 1. Knoedler 1946, pp. 21–22; Aderman et al. 1978, 1, p. 194; Williams 1935, 1, p. 56, illus. facing p. 68.
JAA

18

19

## 20. *Washington Irving* (1783–1859)

Gilbert Stewart Newton (1794–1835)
London, 1830
Oil on canvas
23⅞ x 19¼″
60.6 x 48.9 cm
SS.62.1
Gift in the memory of Mrs. John D. Rockefeller, Jr., by her children

My friend Newton, who sailed from London a few days since took with him a small portrait of me, for which I had sat at request. It is the most accurate likeness that has ever been taken of me.[1]

In 1818 Irving met Gilbert Stuart Newton while in London. Irving, Newton, and Charles Leslie, fast friends all, soon formed the nucleus of a London circle of artists and writers. Irving wrote in a glowing manner one year later:

Newton is the nephew of Stuart, our great portrait painter. He is not so experienced in his art as Leslie, but has uncommon requisites for it. There is a native elegance about everything he does; a delicate taste, a playful fancy, and an extraordinary facility at achieving, without apparent labor or study, what other painters, with the labor and study of years, cannot attain. His eye for color is almost unrivalled, and produces beautiful effects, which have surprised experienced painters, who have been aiming at coloring all their lives. The only danger is, that his uncommon natural advantages may make him remiss in cultivating the more mechanical parts of his art; and he may thus fall short of that preeminent stand in his profession which is completely within his reach, though he cannot fail at all events to become a highly distinguished painter. He is yet but a student in his art, but has produced several admirable portraits."[2]

Newton captured Irving's likeness on at least three occasions. Irving greatly admired a portrait Newton had executed during May, 1820, and held it up as a paradigm when discussing a proposed portrait with Leslie later that year.[3] Newton also created a portrait of the writer for his English publisher, John Murray.[4]

Provenance: Mr. & Mrs. Wentworth Cruger Bacon, Millbrook, NY; Mrs. John D. Rockefeller, Jr., New York City, 1948.

Exhibitions: "The Catskills: Painters, Writers and Tourists in the Mountains 1820–1895," Hudson River Museum of Westchester, Yonkers, NY, 1988–1989; "Washington Irving and His Circle," M. Knoedler and Company, New York City, 1946.

References: 1. Irving 1862–1864, 2, p. 460; 2. Irving 1862–1864, 1, pp. 406–407, 3. Irving 1862–1864, 2, p. 28; 4. Richard Kenin, *Return to Albion, Americans in England 1760–1940*, New York: Holt, Rinehart and Winston, 1979, p. 74, pp. 78–79; *American Collector* 16 (October 1947), p. 8; Joseph T. Butler, "Washington Irving, Romanticism, and Sunnyside: Part I," *Connoisseur* 167 (January 1968), pp. 51–57, illus. p. 12; Butler 1974, pl. 12; Margaret S. Conklin, *Historical Tarrytown and North Tarrytown (A Guide)*, Tarrytown, NY: Tarrytown Historical Society, 1939, p. 56; Groce and Wallace 1957, p. 470; Andrew B. Myers, "Washington Irving and Gilbert Stuart Newton: A *New York Mirror* Contribution Identified," *Bulletin of the New York Public Library* 76 (1972), pp. 237–241; Kenneth Myers, *The Catskills: Painters, Writers and Tourists in the Mountains 1820–1895*, Yonkers, NY: Hudson River Museum of Westchester, 1987, pl. 114; Prown 1956, pp. 110–113; Dunlap 1969, Knoedler 1946, p. 26; Williams 1935. KEJ

## 21. *Napoleon Bonaparte* (1769–1821)

Unknown artist "Rousseau"
Probably Europe, early 19th century
Oil on ivory
8 x 5¾"
20.32 x 14.61 cm
MP.87.183
Gift of J. Dennis Delafield

Napoleon not only conquered the European continent, he dominated its social, architectural, and decorative spheres as well. This Europe, which had been tailored to the French emperor's tastes, captured the imagination of Irving. As the following excerpt from a letter dated 15 July 1805 to his brother Pierre suggests, Irving was captivated by Napoleon:

> By the papers I find that the Emperor is at Fontainebleau, having travelled in coq. [incognito] from Geneva to that place in eighty hours! This is an instance of that promptness, decision, and rapidity that characterize his movements. You may well suppose I am impatient to see this wonderful man, whose life has been a continued series of actions, any one of which would be sufficient to immortalize him.[1]

This portrait on ivory displays a framer's label on the reverse, which reads: Moses Lyon/Manufacturer of gold & silver leaf,/gold & silver bronze/doutist's & gold foil & C/No. 88 Thompson Street/New York.

Provenance: Livingston/Delafield family possession; J. Dennis Delafield, New York City, 1986.

Reference: 1. Aderman et al. 1978, 1, pp. 194–196.
JAA

## 22. *George Washington*

Attributed to James Sharples, Sr. (1751–1811)
Philadelphia, 1796–1811
Pastel on paper
9 x 7"
22.9 x 17.8 cm
VC.79.10

The significance of George Washington in the life of Irving cannot be overemphasized. Beyond the fact that the author was named in honor of the Revolutionary War general and first President, Irving saw Washington as a great source of inspiration throughout his life. By the time he died in 1799, Washington had become an American icon. His heroism in war and his strength in governing were qualities to be emulated. Irving and his contemporaries saw him as no less than the greatest American who ever lived.

As Irving noted in his 1855 preface to his *Life of George Washington*, the general "had very little private life, but was eminently a public character."[1] Irving consistently defended this public character. Many of Irving's earliest public writings during the first decade of the nineteenth century focused on political conflicts between Washington's Federalists and the opposing Jeffersonian Democrats. Irving had, as his nephew Pierre M. Irving later noted, "not the least relish for the asperities of party strife,"[2] but he did strongly defend, often with humor, the Federalist cause in such New York publications as *The Corrector* and the *Evening Post*. These political satires may be seen as a subliminal protection of Washington's legacy and not necessarily as an affirmation of contemporary party views.

Irving's aforementioned biography of Washington was the culmination of his continuing fascination with and admiration for the hero. Historian Stanley T. Williams believed the writing of a Washington biography to be, "from earliest youth,"[3] Irving's greatest dream. As early as 1825, Irving was approached by Archibald Constable, an Edinburgh publisher, to write a biography of George Washington. Irving passed on this offer, but sixteen years later the author began research on his *Life of Washington*. The first two volumes of the biography were published in 1855 by George P. Putnam. Three more volumes completed the series, the last published just before Irving's death in 1859.

English-born artist James Sharples came to the United States in 1793. He and his family toured the country making pastel portraits of famous people. Among the most popular subjects was President George Washington. Portraits like this one originally sold for $15.[4]

Provenance: M. Knoedler and Company, New York City, 1946.

References: 1. Irving 1982, 1, p. 2; 2. Richard Dilworth Rust et al., *The Complete Works of Washington Irving: Miscellaneous Writings, 1803–1859*, Boston: Twayne Publishers, 1981, 1, p. xx; 3. Irving 1982, 1, p. xxv; 4. Butler 1983, p. 24; Aderman et al. 1978, 1, p. xxxvii; Gustavus A. Eisen, *Portraits of Washington*, 3 vols., New York: Robert Hamilton & Associates, 1932, 2, pp. 506–523; *Kennedy Quarterly* 6 (October 1966), p. 140; Katharine McCook Knox, *The Sharples, Their Portraits of George Washington and His Contemporaries, A Diary and an Account of the Life and Work of James Sharples and His Family in England and America*, New Haven: Yale University Press, 1930, pp. 68–69; Sarah B. Sherrill, "Current and Coming," *Antiques* 117 (January 1980), p. 92.
JAA

21

22

## 23. *Bust of Andrew Jackson*
(1767–1845)

William Rush (1756–1833)
Philadelphia, 1819
Plaster
25 x 18 x 10″
63.5 x 45.7 x 25.4 cm
MP.88.250
Gift of J. Dennis Delafield

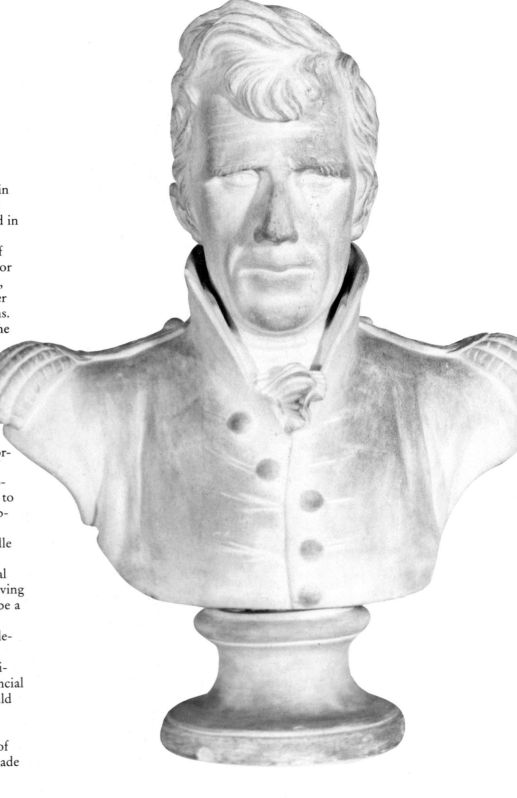

Andrew Jackson was a man of the frontier, born in a rural settlement in the Carolinas in 1767. Although his education was limited, he succeeded in becoming a lawyer. He eventually served as a member of the House of Representatives and briefly as senator from Tennessee. In the War of 1812, Jackson became a national hero after defeating the British at New Orleans. This victory led to his election to the presidency in 1828, an election that was seen as a vindication of the common man.

"An intimate of the President's and a devoted admirer of Jackson," Irving was, at the beginning of Old Hickory's presidency, a great supporter of the Jacksonian party. As the *Boston Post* noted, "with few exceptions, our first literary men belong to the democratic party."[1] Irving's support changed, however, during Jackson's battle with Nicholas Biddle and his Second Bank of the United States. Jackson vetoed congressional renewal of the bank's charter, believing the privately owned institution to be a government-approved monopoly. Irving, as historian Arthur M. Schlesinger, Jr., noted, "deplored the pressure [inflicted by Jackson's policies] on 'the great trading and financial classes,' and concluded that he could no longer go on with so violent an administration."[2]

This head-and-shoulder bust of Jackson in military uniform was made by Philadelphia sculptor William Rush. Rush is known both for his wood carvings and his later terra-cotta and plaster busts of notable figures of his day. Although trained as a ship carver, Rush was both a founding member and frequent exhibitor at the Pennsylvania Academy of the Fine Arts. According to art historian Milo Naeve, this plaster bust of Jackson is the only known surviving cast by Rush of his original 1819 terra-cotta likeness. Presumably casts were made by Rush between 1819 and 1832, and each originally sold for $12. This particular piece was owned by Edward Livingston (1764–1836), a longtime friend of Jackson's, as well as his Secretary of State, and later, minister to France.[3]

Provenance: Livingston/Delafield family possession; J. Dennis Delafield, New York City, 1986.

References: 1, 2. Arthur M. Schlesinger, Jr., *The Age of Jackson*, Boston: Little, Brown & Co., 1946, pp. 238–239, 370; 3. Milo M. Naeve, "William Rush's Terracotta and Plaster Busts of General Andrew Jackson," *The American Art Journal* 21:1 (1989), pp. 18–39; Groce and Wallace 1957, p. 551; Linda Bantel, ed., *William Rush: American Sculptor*, Philadelphia: Pennsylvania Academy of Fine Arts, 1982, pp. 156–158.
JAA

## 24. *Political Friends of Washington Irving*

Attributed to Joseph Jefferson (1829–1905)
Possibly Philadelphia, after 1852
Paper silhouettes mounted on paper
9 9/16 x 13 3/16"
24.3 x 33.5 cm
SS.64.425

The five assembled silhouettes are identified (left to right), "John Tyler/done at/White House/Following the death of/William H. Harrison; Daniel Webster/cut by Joseph Jefferson; John Q. Adams/1767–1848; Franklin Pierce/14th Pres. of U.S.; William H. Harrison/done at McCockran's Fe——,

near 13th Street/Washington, D.C. 1841."

The election in 1840 of "Tippe-canoe and Tyler Too"—William Henry Harrison and John Tyler—greatly surprised Irving. Although he had lost affection for the Jacksonian Democrats, he strongly supported Jackson's heir, Hudson Valley squire and incumbent president Martin Van Buren. At the beginning of Harrison's campaign against fellow New Yorker Van Buren, Irving noted rumors about "General Harrisons [sic] prospects... brightening—I cannot think it possible he should succeed, though the distresses of the country when they press upon the agricultural classes, may be wrested to the disadvantage of [Van Buren's] administration."[1]

Irving had no personal ties to Harrison or Tyler. He did, however, accept appointment to the post of United States Minister to Spain after Tyler's succession to the presidency. Irving's appointment, suggested by Secretary of State Daniel Webster, "was confirmed in the Senate almost by acclamation." Henry Clay, like other frequent opponents of the Tyler administration, "exclaimed: 'Ah, this is a nomination everybody will concur in! If the President would send us such names as this, we should never have any difficulty.'"[2]

These silhouettes belonged to the actor Joseph Jefferson (1829–1905), who was best known for his portrayal of Irving's Rip Van Winkle. Only one of them is identified as having been cut by Jefferson, but his pursuit of this art form is well documented.

Provenance: Joseph Jefferson, Palm Beach, FL; M. Collins.

References: 1. Aderman et al. 1978, 3, p. 38; 2. Aderman et al. 1978, 3, p. 181; Butler 1983, p. 224; *Dictionary of American Biography*, 20 vols., supplement, and index, New York: Charles Scribners' Sons, 1933–1935, 10, pp. 15–17; Frank Freidel, *The Presidents of the United States of America*, White House Historical Association, Washington, DC, 1987, pp. 23–27.
JAA

## 25. *Chancellor Robert R. Livingston* (1746–1813)

Attributed to Gilbert Stuart (1755–1828)
Probably New York, c. 1794
Oil on canvas
35¾ x 26¾"
90.8 x 67.95 cm
MP.87.106
Gift of J. Dennis Delafield

Robert R. Livingston was, as John Adams described, a "downright straight-forward man."[1] He was an instrumental figure in the formation of this country, as well as in creating the political sphere of New York state.

Livingston was the eldest son of Judge Robert R. (1718–1775) and Margaret Beekman Livingston (1724–1800). A graduate of Kings College and a one-time legal partner of John Jay, the United States' first chief justice, Livingston was later appointed Recorder of the City of New York. In 1776, while a member of the Second Continental Congress, Livingston joined Adams, Thomas Jefferson, Benjamin Franklin, and Roger Sherman in preparing the colonies' Declaration of Independence. A year later he was appointed Chancellor of the State of New York. While chancellor, Livingston administered the presidential oath of office to George Washington at his first inaugural in New York City.

In 1801 Livingston accepted the position of United States Minister to France. During his nearly five years as minister, Livingston conducted negotiations for the purchase of the Louisiana Territory. Reflecting on this great land transfer, Livingston noted that "the treaties which we have just signed will cause no tears; ...from this day the United States take their place among the powers of the first rank."[2]

Irving first became acquainted with Livingston while touring Europe in 1804. Irving planned to travel from Nice to Genoa, but found that the French authorities would not allow him to leave the country: apparently his existing passport was of the type that was reserved for "suspicious persons." Irving attempted to clear the matter himself with no success. Finally, after writing to the U.S. Minister in Paris, Livingston, he was granted a new passport and allowed to continue on his journey. Irving believed that if it had not been for Livingston's intervention, his five-week holdover in Nice might have been indefinite. In later years Irving visited the chancellor at his family home, Clermont, along the Hudson River, and dined with his sister, Janet Livingston Montgomery, at Montgomery Place.

Gilbert Stuart was born in North Kingston, Rhode Island. During the American Revolution he studied painting with Benjamin West in London, developing an English portraiture style. Returning to the United States in 1793, Stuart's talent as a painter quickly became well known. This Stuart portrait is one of numerous versions of his c. 1794 portrait of Chancellor Robert Livingston. It was completed for Robert's sister, Janet Livingston Montgomery (1743–1828), widow of the Revolutionary War general and martyr Richard Montgomery.

Provenance: Montgomery/Livingston/Delafield family possession; J. Dennis Delafield, New York City, 1986.

References: 1. Catherine Drinke Bowen, *John Adams and the American Revolution*, Boston: Little, Brown and Company, 1950, p. 462; 2. Joseph Livingston Delafield, *Chancellor Robert R. Livingston of New York and His Family*, New York: American Scenic and Historic Preservation Society, 1911, pp. 322–323; Aderman et al. 1978, 1, pp. 86, 101, 102, 113, 353; Ruth Piwonka, *A Portrait of Livingston Manor 1686–1850*, Germantown, NY: Friends of Clermont, 1986, p. 57.
JAA

26. *William C. Macready*
(1793–1873)
Chester Harding (1792–1866)
England or France, c. 1825
Oil on canvas
25 x 20"
63.5 x 50.8 cm
SS.79.44
Gift of Ronald Tree

The successful English tragedian William C. Macready was well known for his Shakespearean roles, among them that of Macbeth. While playing the Scottish king at the Astor Place Opera House during his 1849 visit to New York, Macready was booed and hissed by a dissatisfied audience. They also showed dissatisfaction in other ways, as Macready's recollection of the occurrence noted: "Copper cents were thrown, some struck me, four or five eggs, a great many apples, nearly—if not quite—a peck of potatoes, lemons, pieces of wood, a bottle of Asafoetida which splashed my own dress, smelling, of course, most horribly."[1]

Irving, along with other prominent citizens, asked him to forgive the occurrence and continue his role, which he did.

Chester Harding engaged in cabinetmaking and sign painting before settling on a career as a portrait painter. During the early years of his career, he specialized in painting prominent Americans. Between 1823 and 1826, Harding worked in England and France, during which time he presumably painted Macready's portrait.

Provenance: M. Knoedler and Company, New York City; Ronald Tree, 1951.

Exhibitions: "Theatrical Evolution: 1776–1976," Hudson River Museum, Yonkers, NY, 1976.

References: 1. Kenneth Spritz, *Theatrical Evolution, 1776–1976*, Yonkers, NY: Hudson River Museum, 1976, p. 29; James T. Flexner, "The Strange Case of Chester Harding," *Antiques* 57 (February 1950), pp. 112–114; Groce and Wallace 1957, pp. 290–91; William Toynbee, editor, *The Diaries of William Charles Macready*, New York: G.P. Putnam's Sons, 1912, 2, p. 423.
JAA

# III Literature And Art

THE CHARACTERS AND SETTINGS in Washington Irving's books have inspired generations of artists to produce paintings, prints, and book illustrations. The close association between Irving and artists can in part be attributed to his literary style. The title of one early work, *The Sketch-Book* (1819), and Irving's choice of the pseudonym Geoffrey Crayon suggest the writer's emphasis on detailed and colorful descriptions of people and places. The most common literary modes employed by young Irving, satire and fantasy, relate to the tradition of English satirical prints of the eighteenth and early nineteenth centuries and to the romantic and fantastic art of the nineteenth century.

Irving displayed an intense personal interest in art. During the first half of the nineteenth century, literary and artistic circles were closely connected; the fledgling American schools of literature and art evolved hand-in-hand. Irving enjoyed the company of countless artist-friends and even toyed with the idea of devoting his talents to art instead of writing.

Some of the works included in this exhibition and catalogue were directly inspired by Irving's literary offerings, *Diedrich Knickerbocker's A History of New-York* (1809), *The Sketch-Book of Geoffrey Crayon, Gent.* (1819), *Life and Voyages of Christopher Columbus* (1828), and *The Alhambra* (1832); others reflect his interest in history and other subjects.

*27. Peter Stuyvesant's Army
Entering New Amsterdam*

William Heath (1795–1840), artist
Sarony & Major, lithographers
New York City, c. 1850
Lithograph
11⅛ x 29¼"
28.3 x 74.3 cm
SS.91.2

In 1809 the young turk Washington
Irving wrote *A History of New-York*,
an imaginative "historical" essay on
New York. Penned under the pseudonym Diedrich Knickerbocker, the
elaborate and intricate composition
mocked the pretensions of the old
Dutch families of New York. The Van
Cortlandts, Stuyvesants, and others
felt the sting of Irving's rapier wit. Irving used his considerable knowledge of
seventeenth-century New York history
to lambast both the early Dutch and
the politics of his own contemporaries.

Irving later regretted that his first
book had acquired the reputation of
being too direct and insulting. He
altered the tone in a revised edition
published in 1851 and included the following half-hearted apology:

At the first appearance of my work,
its aim and drift were misap-
prehended by some of the descendants of the Dutch worthies; and
because I understand that now and
then one may still be found to
regard it with a captious eye. The
far greater part, however, I have
reason to flatter myself, receive my
good-humoured picturings in the
same temper with which they were
executed; and when I find, after a
lapse of nearly forty years, this haphazard production of my youth still
cherished among them; when I find
its very name become a 'household
word,' and used to give the home-
stamp to every thing recommended

for popular acceptation, such as Knickerbocker societies; Knickerbocker insurance companies; Knickerbocker steamboats; Knickerbocker omnibuses; Knickerbocker bread and Knickerbocker ice; and when I find New Yorkers of Dutch descent, priding themselves upon being 'genuine Knickerbockers,' I please myself with the persuasion that I have struck the right chord.[1]

This lithograph served as a large folding plate in the G. P. Putnam author's revised edition and, as noted in the margin, illustrates the passage of Peter Stuyvesant and New Amsterdam's first families into the city.

William Heath was an illustrator who is identified with a group of English artists who trace their roots to political satire. Heath also created six etchings in a grotesque style for the volume *Beauties of Washington Irving, Esq.* (1825).

Provenance: Irving family possession; Louis du Pont Irving, 1945.

References: 1. [Washington Irving] *Diedrich Knickerbocker's A History of New-York*, G. P. Putnam, 1850, pp. 13–14, illus. facing p. 472; *The Beauties of Washington Irving, Esq.*, London: John Bumpus, 1825.
KEJ

## 28. *Mary Philipse* (1730–1825)

Attributed to John Wollaston
(active c. 1733–1769)
New York City, c. 1750
Oil on canvas
29 x 24″
73.7 x 61 cm
PM.80.2
Gift of Mrs. John D. Rockefeller, Jr.

Mary Philipse was a member of a once-powerful faction of Dutch settlers, represented in *A History of New-York*, who did not survive the Revolutionary War as part of New York's elite. Mary Philipse spent much of her life at the manor house in Yonkers and was married there to Roger Morris in 1758. The family remained loyal to the king and so were attainted of treason by the Patriots, forcibly lost their property, and fled to England.

Wollaston captured the likenesses of New Yorkers and other colonials through fairly stock poses. His skill as a drapery painter in England is evidenced in the attention paid to sitters' clothing.

Provenance: Philipse family possession; Mrs. John D. Rockefeller, Jr., New York City.

Exhibitions: Executive Mansion, Albany, NY, 1961–1975; "Divided Loyalties," Philipsburg Manor, North Tarrytown, NY, 1976–1979.

References: Butler 1983, p. 22; Wayne Craven, "John Wollaston: His Career in England and New York City," *American Art Journal* 7 (November 1975), pp. 19–31; William F. Davidson, "Portraits and Landscapes at Philipse Castle," *American Collector* 13 (May 1944), pp. 12–14.
KEJ

**29.** *Eva Margaret Elizabeth DePeyster* (1782–1807)

Charles Willson Peale (1741–1827)
New York City, June 1798
Oil on canvas
29½ x 24½"
74.9 x 62.2 cm
PM.65.861

Miss DePeyster was a New York contemporary of young Irving. The documentation accompanying Peale's portrait of her is remarkable. Peale was related to Eva DePeyster through his second wife, Elizabeth DePeyster Peale, and he and his family visited Mrs. Peale's uncle James DePeyster, his wife, and daughter in New York in 1798. Peale made the following entry in his diary for June 19–29:

I have painted the portraits of Mr. James DePeyster and lady in oil, also ther [sic] portraits in miniature, and as I had Mrs. Peale and the children at their house, and that I might with a better face charge my common price for these portraits, I took advantage of Mrs. DePeyster's absence, and in the time of her being at the Harlem Church I made a likeness of her daughter Sophia [Eva, also called Eliza]...and placed it in the dining room. She was agreeably surprised on seeing it.

I finished these portraits to the entire satisfaction of the family and received for Mr. and Mrs. DePeyster in oil forty dollars each, and seventy dollars for the two miniatures. Eliza I presented to her and she politely presented me with a pair of gold sleeve buttons to wear for her sake.[1]

The Peale scholar Charles Sellers included further biographical information on Miss DePeyster:

Eva Margareta Elizabeth, or simply, to her family circle and friends, Eliza, was the daughter of the James W. DePeysters—"Their only daughter and a great pet," as Peale described her in his autobiography. She had been baptized at Curaçao, May 30, 1784. Her portrait was painted at New York as a surprise gift to her parents, in June, 1798. On Aug. 24, 1805, she married Samuel Hake, Jr., son of a British army commissary of the Revolution.[2]

The painting is signed and dated in the lower right, "C.W. Peale 1798."

Provenance: Miss E.M.E. DePeyster (Mrs. Samuel Hake); her great-nephew Beekman Hunt; Livingston Hunt; M. Knoedler and Company, New York City, 1943.

References: 1., 2. Charles C. Sellers, *Portraits and Miniatures by Charles Willson Peale*, issued as vol. 42, part 1 of the *Transactions of the American Philosophical Society, 1952*, pp. 65, 95; Waldron P. Belknap, Jr., *The De Peyster Genealogy*, Boston: privately printed, 1956, illus. no. 24; Butler 1983, p. 27; William F. Davidson, "Portraits and Landscapes at Philipse Castle," *American Collector* 13 (May 1944), pp. 12–14; Groce and Wallace 1957, p. 492.
KEJ

**30.** *Margaret Beekman Livingston* (1724–1800)

Attributed to Gilbert Stuart (1755–1828)
Probably New York City, c. 1794
Oil on canvas
35 x 27¼"
88.9 x 69.2 cm
MP.88.221
Gift of J. Dennis Delafield

Although Margaret Beekman Livingston did not live to see the publication of *A History of New-York*, in 1809, her portrait symbolizes the world of old New York. Near contemporaries of Mrs. Livingston were scandalized at Irving's irreverent mockery of the venerable old Dutch families:

One lady was pointedly indignant against him, and in an outburst of wrath vowed, if she were a man, she would horsewhip him. The historian was wonderfully amused upon hearing this, and with a degree of modest impudence quite foreign to his natural character, forthwith determined to seek an introduction. He accordingly prevailed on a friend to take him to her house. She received him very stiffly at first, but before the end of the interview he had succeeded in making himself so agreeable that she relaxed entirely from her hauteur, and they became very good friends.[1]

Margaret Beekman Livingston created a stir while sitting for her portrait in Stuart's Manhattan studio. In a letter to her daughter Catharine Livingston Garrettson, Mrs. Livingston wrote that "many gentlemen have been to see the old face and while I was sitting sent up their names and wished to be permitted to come in...everybody says so striking a likeness."[2] Stuart and other copyists created four versions for her daughters.

Provenance: Montgomery/Livingston/Delafield family possession; J. Dennis Delafield, New York City, 1986.

References: 1. Irving 1863, 1, pp. 246–247; 2. Ruth Piwonka, *A Portrait of Livingston Manor, 1686–1850*, Germantown, NY: Friends of Clermont, 1986, p. 59.
KEJ

29

30

ARMS OF VAN CORTLANDT.

G. KANE.

### 31. Van Cortlandt Coat of Arms

G. Kane
Probably New York, 1790–1825
Oil and gold leaf on wooden panel
13¾ x 14″
34.9 x 35.6 cm
VC.58.16

The Van Cortlandts received their share of ribbing in *Diedrich Knickerbocker's A History of New-York*. Oloffe Van Cortlandt (c. 1600–1683/4), the founder of the Van Cortlandt family in America, is portrayed in Irving's satire as "particularly zealous in his devotions to the trencher." His overeating and excessive drinking are ascribed by Irving as the source of his visionary dreams.[1]

American families commissioned coats of arms when they had reached a certain level of economic and social success. G. Kane, whose identity remains elusive, also painted a similar panel bearing the Rockwell coat of arms, currently held in a private collection.

Provenance: Van Cortlandt family possession; Mrs. Robert P. Browne, Garden City, NY, 1958.

References: 1. [Washington Irving] *Diedrich Knickerbocker's A History of New-York*, 2 vols., Philadelphia: Lea & Blanchard, 1809, revised 1839, 1, pp. 126–127; Butler 1967, frontispiece, p. 35; Butler 1983, p. 34.
KEJ

## 32. *Ichabod Crane at a Ball at Van Tassel's Mansion*

John Quidor (1801–1881)
New York, 1855
Oil on canvas
23½ x 34"
59.7 x 86.4 cm
SS.64.556

Gift in memory of Francis P. Garvan,
by his wife Mabel Brady Garvan

And now the sound of the music from the common room, or hall, summoned to the dance.... Ichabod prided himself upon his dancing as much as upon his vocal powers. Not a limb, not a fibre about him was idle; and to have seen his loosely hung frame in full motion, clattering about the room, you would have thought Saint Vitus himself, that blessed patron of the dance, was figuring before you in person.[1]

So Irving described this scene in his story "The Legend of Sleepy Hollow," published as part of *The Sketch-Book of Geoffrey Crayon, Gent.* (1819). The allusion to the graphic artist's tool in the title emphasized the writer's highly visual prose, which in style and subject matter inspired many of American artists including John Quidor. Asher B. Durand, A.D.O. Browere, and Daniel Huntington also depicted incidents from Irving's early works and in doing so participated in the centuries-old European tradition of literary painting. Quidor, who supported himself in large part through decorative painting commissioned by the volunteer fire companies of New York City, expressed an interest in the works of Washington Irving as subject matter during much of his artistic career.

Quidor's depictions of Irving's tales are noteworthy in their marked contrast to more sentimental and strictly illustrative interpretations. Quidor's compositions tend to be very powerful, at times frightening, moving well beyond the intent of the author. The depiction of the party at the home of Crane's beloved Katrina Van Tassel surpasses Irving's description of a lively rustic frolic. Spiritlike farm folk whirl and gyrate before a roaring fire, spurred on by the fiddling of a demonic African-American musician. This figure forms a strong, outwardly moving diagonal at the lower right corner. In the center of the canvas, the angular Ichabod Crane towers over his fellow revelers, cavorting with arms flailing. His dancing partner, the bejeweled Katrina, strikes a balletic pose as she dances on tiptoe. In the foreground, a howling dog and a tipped-over chair are symbols of anarchy. Quidor's use of brown glazes provides the golden aura associated with old master paintings and contributes further to the unearthly quality of the canvas. What is depicted here, the interior of a colonial farmhouse or hell?

"John Quidor/1855/N.Y." is written on the back of the relined canvas and may have been copied from the original inscription.

Modern interest in Quidor has, in some part, made up for the neglect he suffered during his lifetime and immediately after his death. The Brooklyn Museum's landmark exhibition of Quidor's works in 1942 awakened interest in this enigmatic artist.

Provenance: Joseph Harrison, Jr.; Thomas B. Clarke; Mabel Brady Garvan, New York City, 1951.

Exhibitions: Pennsylvania Academy of Fine Arts, Philadelphia, PA, 1857; "John Quidor, 1801–1881," The Brooklyn Museum, Brooklyn, NY, 1942; "Washington Irving and His Circle," M. Knoedler and Company, New York City, 1946; "Rediscoveries in American Art," Cincinnati Art Museum, Cincinnati, OH, 1955; "Art Across America," Munson Williams Proctor Institute, Utica, NY, 1960; "Art in New York State: The River, People and Places," New York World's Fair, New York City, 1964; "John Quidor," Whitney Museum of American Art, New York City, 1966; "Painter of American Legend," Wichita Art Museum and University of Wisconsin-Milwaukee, 1973; "Washington Irving of Sunnyside: A Bicentennial Sketch," National Portrait Gallery, Washington, DC, 1983; "New Horizons: American Painting 1840–1910," Smithsonian Institution Traveling Exhibition Service, Washington, DC, 1987–1988.

References: 1. [Washington Irving] *The Sketch-Book of Geoffrey Crayon, Gent.*, second edition, 2 vols., London: John Murray, 2, pp. 338–339; *Art Across America*, Utica, NY: Munson Williams Proctor Institute, 1960, no. 39; John I.H. Baur, *John Quidor, 1801–1881*, Brooklyn, NY: The Brooklyn Museum, 1942, no. 10; Butler 1983, p. 204; Butler 1974, pl. 10; *Catalogue of Pictures, Statuary, and Bronzes of John Harrison, Jr.*, Philadelphia: Rittenhouse Square, 1870, no. 26; Chad Mandeles, "A New Look at John Quidor's Leatherstocking Paintings," *American Art Journal* 12 (Summer 1980), pp. 65–74; *New Horizons: American Painting 1840–1910* (text is in Russian), Moscow: The Minister of Art of the Soviet Union, 1987, illus. no. 29; *Paintings, Statuary, etc. The Remainder of the Collection of Joseph Harrison, Jr.... and Belonging to the Estate of Mrs. Sarah Harrison*, Philadelphia: Philadelphia Art Galleries, 1912, listed no. 38; Prown 1956, fig. 34; David M. Sokol, "John Quidor, Literary Painter," *American Art Journal* 2 (Spring 1970), pp. 60–73; David M. Sokol, "John Quidor and the Literary Sources for His Paintings," *Antiques* 102 (October 1972), pp. 675–679; David M. Sokol, "The Curious World of John Quidor," *Antiques World* 3 (October 1981), pp. 46–50; David M. Sokol, "John Quidor—An Important Exhibition," *Connoisseur* 184 (November 1973), pp. 202–204; Sokol 1973, p. 27; Knoedler 1946, p. 30.
KEJ

## 33. *Courtship in Sleepy Hollow: Ichabod Crane and Katrina Van Tassel*

John Rogers (1829–1904)
New York City
After August 25, 1865 (patent date)
13¹⁵⁄₁₆ x 13⅛ x 7½"
35.4 x 33.3 x 19.1 cm
SS.64.73

Mass-produced sculptured groups designed by John Rogers served as affordable statuary for America's middle class. Rogers, a sculptor who had trained in Paris and Rome, established a studio in New York City in 1859. For the next thirty-five years, he produced over eighty genre groups that were cast in porcelain and plaster by the thousands.[1]

Provenance: Unknown.

Exhibition: "Nineteenth-century American Paintings From Private Collections," Hudson River Museum, Yonkers, NY, 1974.

References: 1. Groce and Wallace 1957, p. 544; Chetwood Smith, *Rogers Groups*, Boston: Goodshead, 1934, p. 55.
KEJ

## 34. *Ichabod Crane and Katrina Van Tassel*

Daniel Huntington (1816–1906)
New York City, 1861
Oil on canvas
29⅝ x 24¼″
75.2 x 61.6 cm
PM.71.2

> When he entered the house, the conquest of his heart was complete....Here, rows of resplendent pewter, ranged on a long dresser, dazzled his eyes. In one corner stood a huge bag of wool ready to be spun; in another a quantity of linsey-woolsey just from the loom; ears of Indian corn and strings of dried apples and peaches, hung in gay festoons along the walls, mingled with the gaud of red peppers;. ...From the moment Ichabod laid his eyes upon these regions of delight, the peace of his mind was at an end, and his only study was how to gain the affections of the peerless daughter of Van Tassel.[1]

A student of Samuel F. B. Morse and Henry Inman, Daniel Huntington was a highly successful portraitist and genre painter, who served as president of the National Academy of Design, 1862–1869 and 1877–1891. Huntington was praised for this painting and other efforts,[2] including this assessment of his portrayal of the above-excerpted scene from "The Legend of Sleepy Hollow":

> The contrast between the ignorant Dutch beauty, coquettish to the plumb little fingers' ends, and the exeedingly learned schoolmaster, knowing nothing about woman except to praise her, is so wonderfully told in this picture that we almost fancy we should have been able to decipher Ichabod's melancholy future had we never read Irving. It is hardly possible to avoid caricature, as Huntington has done, and yet write in multitudinous, unmistakable lines of idiosyncrasy on faces and figures. We wish we had space to refer at large to the elaboration of accessories in the Dutch kitchen, but must simply say that in all respects this picture is one of the best genre pictures ever produced here.[3]

The painting is signed in the lower left "D. Huntington, 1861."

Provenance: Vanderbilt Webb and William H. Osborn, New York City, 1951.

References: 1. [Washington Irving] *The Sketch-Book of Geoffrey Crayon, Gent.*, 2 vols., London: John Murray, 2, pp. 367–368; 2. Groce and Wallace 1957, p. 335; 3. G. W. Sheldon, *American Painters: With One Hundred and Four Examples of Their Work Engraved on Wood*, enlarged edition, New York: Appleton and Company, 1881, pp. 107–109; Butler 1983, illus. p. 220; Marshall B. Davidson, *The American Heritage History of the Writers' America*, New York: American Heritage Publishing Company, 1973, p. 115; Agnes Gilchrist, "Daniel Huntington, portrait painter over seven decades," *Antiques* 87 (June 1965), pp. 709–711; Keller 1976, p. 222; Prown 1956, fig. 36; Henry T. Tuckerman, *Book of the Artists, American Artist Life, Comprising Biographical and Critical Sketches of American Artists: Preceded by an Historical Account of the Rise and Progress of Art in America*, New York: G.P. Putnam, 1867, p. 331.
KEJ

## 35. *Headless Horseman of Sleepy Hollow*

George Washington Allston Jenkins
(1816–1907)
New York City, 1840–1865
Oil on canvas
26 x 36⅛"
66 x 91.8 cm
SS.64.538
Gift of Benjamin G. Jenkins

> But this was no time for petty fears;
> the goblin was hard on his
> haunches; and (unskilful rider that
> he was!) he had much-ado to main-
> tain his seat; sometimes slipping on
> one side, and sometimes jolted on
> the high ridge of his horse's back
> bone, with a violence that he verily
> feared would cleave him asunder.[1]

The nightmarish scene of Ichabod
Crane pursued by the Headless Horseman (in actuality his rival Brom Bones)
as depicted by Jenkins owes much to
the highly visual description of the
chase in Irving's tale and includes
details ranging from the "starvelling
ribs" of Crane's mount, Gunpowder,
to the shadowy image of the Old
Dutch Church barely visible in the
background.

Jenkins, who exhibited at the
National Academy of Design between
1842 and 1865, was a portraitist and
genre painter. The canvas is inscribed,
on the reverse: "Headless Horseman of
Sleepy Hollow by George W.A.
Jenkins."

Provenance: Lawrence Waters Jenkins,
Salem, MA; Benjamin G. Jenkins, Weston,
MA, 1945.

References: [1] [Washington Irving] *The
Sketch-Book of Geoffrey Crayon, Gent.*,
second edition, 2 vols., London: John
Murray, 2, p. 405; Butler 1983, p. 198;
Groce and Wallace 1957, p. 348; George S.
Hellman, "Washington Irving," *American
Collector* 16:9 (October 1947), pp. 10–12,
53.
KEJ

## 36. *Ichabod Crane, Respectfully Dedicated to Washington Irving*

William J. Wilgus (1819–1853), artist
C. E. Lewis, lithographer
Mooney & Buell, printer
A.W. Wilgus, publisher
Buffalo, New York, c. 1856
Chromolithograph
13⅝ x 19½"
33.4 x 49.5 cm
SS.91.1

> "If I could but reach that bridge"
> thought Ichabod "I am safe." Just
> then he heard the black steed pant-
> ing and blowing close behind him,
> he even fancied he felt his hot
> breath. Just then he saw the goblin
> rising in his stirrups and in the very
> act of hurling his head at him.

This quotation is reproduced on
the lithograph to underscore the terror
Ichabod Crane experiences as he
attempts to outride the Headless
Horseman of Sleepy Hollow.

Sixteen-year-old William John
Wilgus confounded the National Academy of Design when he exhibited the
first version of this painting, now in
the collection of the National Gallery
of Art, in the annual exhibition of
1835. A reviewer of the exhibition in
New York's *Evening Star* lauded the
artist's "extraordinary degree of con-
ception and boldness of execution."
Charles Viele has argued that a mature
Wilgus created a second version,
which served as the basis for this chromolithograph. Its present location is
unknown.[1]

Wilgus had studied with Samuel
F. B. Morse during the mid-1830s and
remained in New York City until 1841
or so when he moved to Buffalo.

The chromolithograph also bears
the following inscription: "Entered
according to Act of Congress 1856
Office of the Northern District New
York."

Provenance: Guild House, Tarrytown, NY,
1946.

References: 1. Charles Viele, "Two headless horsemen of Sleepy Hollow," *Antiques*
114:5 (November 1978), pp. 1042–1043;
Groce and Wallace 1957, p. 686.
KEJ

35

36

## 37. *Joseph Jefferson as "Rip Van Winkle"* (1829–1905)

George Waters (1839–1912)
New York, 1871
Oil on canvas
37½ x 28¾"
95.3 x 73 cm
SS.79.7

The actor Joseph Jefferson first played Rip Van Winkle on stage in 1865; he became so closely identified with the part that he appeared in the role for decades and through a series of international tours. It was considered a necessary part of every child's education to see Jefferson on stage in the Dion Boucicault version of *Rip Van Winkle*.[1]

Waters, a New York State artist who had studied in Munich and Dresden, served as art director at Elmira College of Art.[2] A similar canvas by Andrew MacNair (b. 1828) is in the collection of the New York State Bridge Authority.[3]

The painting is signed and dated in the lower right.

Provenance: Louis du Pont Irving, Tarrytown, NY, 1945.

Exhibitions: "Theatrical Evolution: 1776–1976," Hudson River Museum, Yonkers, NY, 1976; "Illustrated Editions of 'Rip Van Winkle,'" Wilson Art Center, the Harley School, Rochester, NY, 1978; Arnot Art Museum, Elmira, NY, 1979.

References: 1. *Dictionary of American Biography*, 20 vols., supplement and index, New York: Charles Scribner's Sons, 1933–1935, 10, pp. 15–17; 2. Groce and Wallace 1957, p. 664; 3. Personal correspondence, John S. Stillman, Chairman New York State Bridge Authority, to Joseph T. Butler, Curator, Sleepy Hollow Restorations, July 7, 1983; Butler 1983, p. 207; *Mantel Fielding's Dictionary of American Painters, Sculptors, and Engravers*, compiled by James F. Carr, New York: James F. Carr, 1965, p. 393; Douglas C. McKenzie, "The Acting of Joseph Jefferson III," Ph.D. dissertation, University of Oregon, 1973, p. 36.
KEJ

## 38. Set of drawings for "Rip Van Winkle"

Felix Octavius Carr Darley (1822–1888)
New York City, c. 1848
Ink and watercolor on paper
8⅞ x 10⅞"
22.5 x 27.6 cm
SS.64.557–SS.64.562

In 1848 and 1849 respectively, the American Art-Union, a national association for the promotion of art in the United States, sent each of its subscribers a set of six etched lithographs and accompanying texts for the stories "Rip Van Winkle" and "The Legend of Sleepy Hollow." Darley provided the original drawings, which were rendered in outline as lithographs. This set of drawings for "Rip Van Winkle" appears to have been watercolored in the nineteenth century.

See entry 40 for biographical information on Darley and further references.

Provenance: Old Print Shop, New York City, 1961.

Exhibitions: "The Catskills: Painters, Writers, and Tourists in the Mountains 1820–1895," Hudson River Museum of Westchester, Yonkers, NY, 1988–1989; "The Hudson Heritage: Time, Man and the River," Hudson River Museum, Yonkers, NY, 1977.

References: Theodore Bolton, "The Book Illustrations of Felix O.C. Darley," *Proceedings of the American Antiquarian Society* 61 (April 1951), pp. 137–182, p. 155; *...illustrated by Darley* 1978, figs. 29, 30; *Illustrations of Rip Van Winkle, Designed and Etched by Felix O.C. Darley, for the Members of the American Art-Union*, 1849; Washington Irving, *Rip Van Winkle and the Legend of Sleepy Hollow*, Tarrytown, NY: Sleepy Hollow Restorations, 1974, lithographs reprinted; Koke 1982, 1, fig. 429; Maybelle Mann, *The American Art-Union*, Otisville, NY: ALM Associates, 1977, pls. 1–6; Kenneth S. Myers, *The Catskills: Painters, Writers, and Tourists in the Mountains 1820–1895*, Yonkers, NY: Hudson River Museum of Westchester, 1987, SS.64.557 illus. pp. 124–125, SS.64.560 illus. pl.9; *Old Print Shop Portfolio* 23:7 (March 1964) SS.64.558, illus. p. 163.
KEJ

37

38

38

38

38

**39. Drawings for *The Sketch-Book***

Augustus Hoppin (1828–1896)
George Loring Brown (1814–1889)
William J. Hennessey (1839–1917)
Henry W. (1824–?) or William F.
Herrick
Pencil and gouache on wood (probably
boxwood)
United States
Mid to late nineteenth century
3⅝ x 3¼ x ⅞ to 2½ x 5⅝ x ⅞"
8 x 8.3 x .4 cm to 6.4 x 13.1 x .4 cm
SS.80.40

These four woodblocks bear designs
for engravings that were never executed. Sketched in pencil on a gouache
ground coating, the scenes, illustrating
stories in *The Sketch-Book*, are rare
survivors that document the process of
book illustration during the nineteenth
century. They include a half-length,
profile sketch of an elderly Rip Van
Winkle carrying the figure of Father
Time on his shoulders; an illustration
of "The Wife," depicting a woman
greeting two men at the gate, which is

inscribed "Herrick Del" in the lower
right corner, a view of Irving resting in
the inn parlor, taken from "Stratford-
on-Avon," and signed in reverse in the
lower right corner, "Hennesssey
Del."; a romantic vignette of two men
surrounded by a pack of dogs in front
of the old family mansion, to illustrate
"Christmas Eve," signed in reverse in
the lower left corner, "G.L. Brown."

Although the drawing of Rip Van
Winkle is not signed, it is accompanied
by an inscription label "Drawn by
Augustis [sic] Hoppin, Providence,
R.I." All of the artists were painters,
illustrators, and wood engravers.

Provenance: Unknown

Exhibition: "Washington Irving," Grolier
Club, New York City, 1983.

References: Groce and Wallace 1957, pp.
85–86, 308, 310–311, 326–327; *Mantel
Fielding's Dictionary of American Painters,
Sculptors, and Engravers*, compiled by
James F. Carr, New York: James F. Carr,
1965, pp. 44, 165, 167, 175.
KEJ

**40. Drawings for *The Alhambra***

Felix Octavius Carr Darley (1822–1888)
New York City, c. 1851
Ink wash on paper
8½ x 6¼" to 7¼ x 5⅛"
21.6 x 15.9 cm to 18.4 x 13 cm
SS.63.35, SS.63.36, SS.63.40–.41

Felix O.C. Darley provided illustrations for a series of author-revised
editions of Irving's works published by
G.P. Putnam between 1848 and 1851.
In 1829 Irving had resided in the
Alhambra at Granada; he is credited
with the reawakening of international
interest in the Moorish monument and
assuring its preservation.

The ink-wash drawing entitled
"The Alhambra," published as a title
page, captures the romantic anticipa-
tion felt by Irving and other first-time
visitors. Several gateways are mentioned in the early pages of the book,
including the Gate of Charles V, the
Gate of Justice, and the entrance to the
Court of Alberca. Illustrations of the
episodes "Aben Habuz, the Arabian

Astrologer, and the Christian Princess" and "The Crusade of the Grand Master of the Alcantera" testify to Darley's skill as a draughtsman and in depicting action scenes. More recent Spanish history is illustrated in the sketches of Spanish dancers, observed by Irving as he journeys to the palace, as well as a scene of confrontation and violence from the "Governor and the Notary." All are signed "F.O.C. Darley."

Darley ranked as one of America's premier book and magazine illustrators during the mid-nineteenth century. Born in Philadelphia, he spent much of his early career in New York City where he gained fame for his illustrations of the literary works of James Fenimore Cooper and Irving. Darley was elected to the National Academy of Design in 1852 and moved to Delaware upon his marriage in 1859.

Provenance: Irving family possession; Louis du Pont Irving, 1945.

Exhibitions: "…illustrated by Darley: an exhibition of original drawings by the American book illustrator Felix O.C. Darley, 1822–1888," Delaware Art Museum, Wilmington, DE, 1978; "The Bicentenary of the Birth of Washington Irving," Columbia University Library, New York City, 1983.

References: Theodore Bolton, "The Book Illustrations of Felix Octavius Carr Darley," *Proceedings of the American Antiquarian Society* 61 (April 1951), pp. 137–182; Butler 1983, p. 216; Butler 1974, p. 19; Groce and Wallace 1957, p. 165; *…illustrated by Darley* 1978, figs. 41 and 42; Ethel King, *Darley, The Most Popular Illustrator of His Time*, Brooklyn, NY: Theo Gaus' Sons, Inc., 1964; Myers 1974, fig. 88; Frank Weitenkamf, "F.O.C. Darley, American Illustrator, *Art Quarterly* 10 (Spring 1947), pp. 100–113.
KEJ

## 41. *Columbus at the Court of Ferdinand and Isabella*

Abraham Woodside (1819–1853)
Philadelphia, 1846
Oil on canvas
44 x 54½"
111.8 x 138.4 cm
PM.71.1

To receive with suitable pomp and distinction, the Sovereigns had ordered their throne to be placed in public, under a rich canopy of brocade of gold in a vast and splendid salon. Here the King and Queen awaited his arrival, seated in state …attended by the dignitaries of their Court, and the principal nobility of Castile, Valentia, Catalonia, and Arragon….As Columbus approached, the Sovereigns arose….Bending his knees, he requested to kiss their hands; but there was some hesitation on the part of their Majesties to permit this act of vassalage. Raising him in the most gracious manner, they ordered him to seat himself in their presence; a rare honour in this proud and punctilious court.[1]

Irving's fascination with Spanish history and culture was first expressed in his writings in the above-quoted *The Life and Voyages of Columbus* (1828). He further explored the subject in *The Conquest of Granada* (1829) and *The Alhambra* (1832). Irving's reverence for Spanish culture was deeply appreciated during his lifetime; he served as the United States's first Spanish-speaking Minister to Spain between 1842 and 1846.

This portrayal of the Spanish court welcoming Columbus shares similarities in setting and placement of figures with Emanuel Leutze's more skilled *Ferdinand Removing the Chains from Columbus* (1843). Where clothed, Woodside's doll-like people wear fashions more in keeping with the nineteenth rather than the fifteenth century. The native Americans and pile of nature's riches serve as obvious symbols of the New World. Woodside signed and dated this canvas in the lower left corner.

Abraham Woodside not only painted portraits and religious, historical, and allegorical scenes, he earned extra income by decorating fire engines. He exhibited at the Pennsylvania Academy, the Maryland Historical Society, and the American Art-Union.[2]

Provenance: C.H. Rogers; M. Knoedler and Company, New York, 1949.

Exhibition: "Washington Irving and His Circle," M. Knoedler and Company, New York City, 1946.

References: 1. Washington Irving, *History of the Life and Voyages of Christopher Columbus*, second edition, 2 vols., New York: G. & C. & H. Carvill, 1831, 1, p. 179; 2. Groce and Wallace 1957, p. 701; William H. Gerdts, "Belshazzar's Feast II: 'That is his shroud'," *Art in America* 61:3 (May-June 1973), pp. 58–65; Knoedler 1946, p. 32.
KEJ

## 42. *George Washington at Yorktown*

Attributed to James Peale (1749–1831)
United States, after 1782
Oil on canvas
26½ x 35½"
67.3 x 90.2 cm
VC.80.8

The Peale family created seemingly countless portraits of Washington. This version, showing George Washington at Yorktown, with a vignette to his right containing a battle at sea and a distinctive windmill associated with Yorktown Heights, Virginia, is attributed stylistically to James Peale.

Irving's lifelong fascination with his namesake, George Washington, culminated fittingly in his last literary effort, the five-volume *Life of George Washington*, published between 1855 and 1859.

Provenance: Mrs. Johanna Lloyd (traditionally received from George Washington); Colonel William Hindman, Dorchester County, MD; his niece, Mrs. Maria Campbell Winchester, and her great-granddaughter, Miss Elsie Bond, Baltimore, MD; M. Knoedler and Company, New York City, 1949.

Exhibitions: "Portraits of George Washington and other Eighteenth-century Americans," M. Knoedler and Company, New York City, 1939; "Washington Irving and his Circle," M. Knoedler and Company, New York City, 1946; Executive Mansion, Albany, NY, 1961–1975; "Divided Loyalties," Philipsburg Manor, North Tarrytown, NY, 1976–1979.

References: Gustavus A. Eisen, *Portraits of Washington*, 3 vols., New York: Robert Hamilton & Associates, 1932, p. 306; Groce and Wallace 1957, pp. 492–493; Charles C. Sellers, *Portraits and Miniatures by Charles Willson Peale*, issued as vol. 42, Part 1 of the *Transactions of the American Philosophical Society, 1952*, p. 217; *Portraits of George Washington and other Eighteenth-Century Americans*, New York: M. Knoedler and Company, 1939, no. 5; Knoedler 1946, no. 2.
KEJ

# *IV* Sunnyside

SUNNYSIDE, THE ROMANTIC-STYLE cottage near the Hudson River remodeled by Washington Irving, is a visual autobiography of the writer. Irving envisioned it as a "little snuggery" where he could enjoy the comfortable life of a country gentleman. Purchased and renovated from the mid-1830s, the two-room tenant farmhouse reflects Irving's creativity both as a writer and as an amateur architect.

The Dutch-inspired stepped gables, which still dominate the house, are significant not only as early examples of American architectural Romanticism but also as tribute to Irving's first great work, *Diedrich Knickerbocker's A History of New-York* (1809). This parody of New York's original Dutch settlers secured for Irving a lifelong reputation as a satirist, and so it is fitting that a Dutch motif should be a dominant feature of the cottage's exterior.

In 1847, more than ten years after the original Dutch scheme was completed, Irving added a Spanish tower. Its design memorialized his years—1842 to 1846—as Envoy Extraordinary and Minister Plenipotentiary to the Court of Queen Isabella II of Spain.

The interior of the house also visually illustrates Irving's life and talents. His famous study, with its alcove containing a divan and hung with draperies of Turkey red fabric, attested to the author's preference for the multifunction rooms that he used while he lived abroad. Similar alcoves in a guest room on the second floor of the house were reminiscent of apartments familiar to Irving during his European travels in the first decade of the nineteenth century. The striped wallpaper in one of these spaces, specifically chosen by Irving, created a tentlike atmosphere similar to French interiors designed by Percier and Fontaine.

During and after his lifetime, Irving's Sunnyside captured the imagination of artists, fellow authors, and admirers. As the various works included in this section suggest, Sunnyside was seen throughout most of the century as an Irving creation as significant and admired as Rip Van Winkle or Ichabod Crane.

### 43. *Sunnyside*

George Inness (1825–1896)
Probably New York, 1850–1860
Oil on canvas
14¾ x 19¾"
37.5 x 50.2 cm
SS.79.34

There may be no image truer to Irving's own view of Sunnyside than this depiction by New York artist George Inness. Although the viewer's first impression is that the lush landscape almost overwhelms the author's "little snuggery," the portrayal of the house and its setting is faithful. Inness has captured the romantic and idyllic image that Irving described in an 1853 letter: "grass is growing up to my door,–the roses and honeysuckles are clambering about my windows, the acacias and liburnums are in full flower, singing birds have built in the ivy against the wall...Nature is in full dress."[1]

Irving's Sunnyside was not so much a house in nature as it was a part of nature. The author's intent of creating a cottage that looked as if it had evolved with the landscape exemplified the writings of such noted nineteenth-century American tastemakers as Alexander Jackson Downing (1815–1852) and Gervase Wheeler. Both men codified the English-born Romantic style in architecture and landscape design;

Downing applauded Sunnyside, both house and garden, as an example of successful design.

George Inness grew up in New York City and near Newark, New Jersey. His early painting style was greatly influenced by the realism of the Hudson River School. However, numerous trips to Europe provided Inness with other inspirations and, as a result, a greater individuality, as this lyrical landscape suggests. The artist's selection of Sunnyside as subject matter illustrates the popularity of both Irving and his country cottage. This painting was probably done at Sunnyside in the 1850s.

Provenance: Williams and Everett Galleries, Boston; Thomas Wigglesworth, Boston; his great-niece, Mrs. James H. Beale, Boston; Robert C. Vose, Jr., Boston; Robert C. Vose III and Abbot William Vose, Boston; Vose Galleries, Boston, 1945; M. Knoedler and Company, New York City, 1946.

Exhibitions: Museum of Fine Arts, Boston, 1920–1928; "Washington Irving and His Circle," M. Knoedler and Company, New York City, 1946; Executive Mansion, Albany, NY, 1961–1975, "Art and the Excited Spirit, America in the Romantic Period," Ann Arbor, MI, 1972; "American Painting Around 1850," Utah Museum of Fine Arts, Salt Lake City, 1976; "The

Gothic Revival Style in America, 1830–1870," Museum of Fine Arts, Houston, TX, 1976; "New York, the State of Art," New York State Museum, Albany, NY, 1977.

References: 1. Aderman et al. 1982, 4, p. 406; *Art and the Excited Spirit, America in the Romantic Period*, Ann Arbor: University of Michigan Museum of Art, 1972, no. 100; *Art in New York State: The River, Places and People*, Buffalo, NY: The Buffalo Fine Arts Academy, 1964, fig. 48; Butler 1983, p. 201; Joseph T. Butler, "Washington Irving, Romanticism, and Sunnyside: Part I," *Connoisseur* 167 (January 1968), pp. 51–57, illus. no. 11; Butler 1974, p. 36; Groce and Wallace 1957, pp. 340–341; Katherine S. Howe, "Product of an Age: The Gothic Revival in the United States," *Nineteenth Century* 3 (Spring 1977), pp. 62–71, illus. p. 78; Katherine S. Howe and David B. Warren, *The Gothic Revival Style in America, 1830–1870*, Houston, TX: The Museum of Fine Arts, 1976, no. 170; LeRoy Ireland, *The Works of George Inness, An Illustrated Catalogue Raisonne*, Austin, TX: University of Texas Press, 1965, no. 60; Keller 1976, p. 246; *Kennedy Quarterly* 8 (September 1968), p. 104; Knoedler 1946, p. 44; Robert S. Olpin, *American Painting Around 1850*, Salt Lake City, UT: University of Utah, 1976, no. 15; *What is American in American Art*, New York: M. Knoedler and Company, 1971, no. 49.
JAA

## 44. *The Old Cottage Taken Previous to Improvement*

Attributed to George Harvey
(c. 1800/01–1878)
New York, 1835
Watercolor on paper
8¼ x 12¼"
21.0 x 31.1 cm
SS.80.17

George Harvey's 1835 watercolor records the old Dutch farmhouse prior to expansion by its new owner, Washington Irving. The house, which had been occupied by members of the Acker and Van Tassel families, was reminiscent of Lowlands vernacular architecture. This connection with the Dutch colonization of the region must have been a particularly attractive feature to Irving, who had a lifelong interest in local history.

Although he made many alterations to the two-room stone cottage, Irving was sensitive to its historical style. He emphasized the Dutch inspiration, adding stepped gables and antique weathervanes. He also incorporated into the building's façade the year 1656, which he believed to be the date of the original construction.

Born in England, Harvey settled in the United States, painting in New York and Boston. He became famous for both his still-life paintings and landscapes. Harvey was a close friend of Irving's and oversaw much of the architectural renovation of Sunnyside. He returned to England sometime after 1840, where he died in 1878.

Provenance: Irving family possession; Louis du Pont Irving, 1945.

References: Butler 1983, p. 211; Butler 1974, pl. 22; Groce and Wallace 1957, p. 298; Harvey 1850; Terry B. Morton, "What good is a Poet's House?" *Historic Preservation* 12 (1960), p. 42; Keller 1976, p. 225; Donald A. Shelley, "George Harvey, English Painter of Atmospheric Landscapes in America," *American Collector* 17 (April 1948), pp. 10–13.
JAA

**45.** *Plan of Proposed Alterations to-the-Property of Washington-Irving-Esquire-at-Tarrytown-River Front*

Calvin Pollard (1797–1850)
New York City, July 1835
Watercolor and ink on paper
15³⁄₁₆ x 20⅞″
38.6 x 50.6 cm
SS.80.29

Even though there is no record that Irving engaged the prominent New York architect and draftsman Calvin Pollard in the renovation of his cottage, this drawing of the river side, as well as one of the southern, or front, façade, and an accompanying floor plan suggest that Pollard was consulted at the beginning of Irving's building project. They are dated the summer of 1835, soon after Irving had acquired the Van Tassel cottage.

Although there are similarities between Pollard's scheme and that which Irving and George Harvey created—mainly the Dutch-inspired stepped gables, there are also strong differences. In comparing this elevation with Harvey's own *Scudding Clouds...*(no. 46), the viewer will note that Harvey's design for the main core of the house retained the original cottage's horizontal proportions: Pollard's proposal extends the river wall, which most assuredly would have added to the cost of the project. Harvey worked with the existing central chimney and window configurations of the Van Tassel cottage, whereas Pollard sketched more elaborate arrangements. Perhaps Pollard's scheme was judged too costly by Irving, whose later additions and changes to the house were tightly budgeted.

Provenance: Irving family possession; Louis du Pont Irving, 1945.

References: Butler 1983, p. 212; Harold D. Cater, "Washington Irving and Sunnyside," *New York History* 38 (April 1957), pp. 135–136.
JAA

**46.** *Scudding Clouds After A Shower/The Residence of Washington Irving Esqr.*

George Harvey (c.1800/01–1878)
New York, 1836–1840
Watercolor on paper
8¼ x 13⅝″
21 x 34.6 cm
SS.79.22

Sunnyside was a frequent subject of George Harvey's paintings. His watercolors and oils document the evolution of the house, which he designed with Irving. This particularly beautiful rendering shows the house from the river side, before the intrusion of the railroad. The Gothic Revival–style veranda, visible at the left, shelters an open door to Irving's parlor. The veranda was often the scene of family gatherings, and Irving himself liked to pull his favorite chair outside to sit and enjoy the view of the Tappan Zee.

The bluish-green-and-white striped awnings visible on two of the second-floor windows were considered an innovation at that time. Irving had seen similar treatments in Europe during his travels. He told one admirer that these unusual exterior treatments were made of "tent cloth...[which he] had to order...from France as none was to be procured in New York."[1]

In describing this picture, Harvey noted that Irving had admired the artist's own nearby Elizabethan-style residence and at Sunnyside "desired something similar, but modified by Dutch roofs,"[2] referring to stepped gables.

Provenance: Kennedy Galleries, New York City, 1946.

Exhibition: "One Hundred Years Ago in North America, An Exhibition of Water Color Drawings by George Harvey," A.N.A., Kennedy Galleries, New York City, 1940.

References: 1. Aderman et al. 1982, 3, p. 15; 2. Butler, 1983, p. 213; Joseph T. Butler, "Washington Irving, Romanticism, and Sunnyside: Part I," *Connoisseur* 167 (January 1968), pp. 51–57; Butler 1974, no. 34; Groce and Wallace 1957, p. 298; Harvey 1850, p. 17, no. 10; Myers 1974, p. 79; Donald A. Shelley, "George Harvey, English Painter of Atmospheric Landscapes in America," *American Collector* 17 (April 1948), pp. 10–13.
JAA

45

46

## 47. Weathervane

Probably the Netherlands, 1765
Copper
12⅛ x 20½"
30.8 x 52.1 cm
SS.64.419

Perhaps Irving's interest in the Dutch colonization of the Hudson region led to his inclusion of this pennant-and-dove weathervane on the tower of Sunnyside. The copper vane, dated 1765, was given to Irving by Gill Davis, whom the author described as the "King of Coney Island." Irving wrote that Davis had retrieved the vane from a demolished windmill in Rotterdam.

Irving welcomed the addition of the weathervane, in particular because he had found his recently completed tower lacking a final touch. He was forced to admit that the cupola on the tower was the "only part of it that is not adapted to some valuable purpose...[and] which has no bell in it and is about as serviceable as the feather in one's cap."[1]

The pennant weathervane, as well as the other vanes collected by the author and used elsewhere on the house, are visible in many of the paintings included in this section. A reproduction of this particular weathervane has been installed on the tower.

Provenance: Irving family possession; Louis du Pont Irving, 1945.

References: 1. Aderman et al. 1982, 4, pp. 138–139; Butler 1974, pp. 66–67; Butler 1983, p. 274; Mabel M. Swan, "On Weather Vanes," *Antiques* 23 (February 1933),
pp. 64–65.
JAA

## 48. *Washington Irving and His Little Dog*

Felix Octavius Carr Darley (1822–1888)
New York City, July 1848
Pencil on paper
8⅞ x 11⅞"
22.5 x 30.2 cm
SS.64.543

A retired Irving is shown with "his little dog" at Sunnyside relaxing against what appears to be a grouping of rocks. The author had numerous animals at the cottage, among them dogs. Irving described one pet's greeting on a homecoming in 1853, "my little terrier slut Ginger, bounded about me almost crazy with delight, having five little Gingers toddling at her heels, with which she had enriched me during my absence."[1]

Provenance: Bland Gallery, Inc., New York City, 1946.

Exhibition: "Washington Irving of Sunnyside: A Bicentennial Sketch," National Portrait Gallery, Washington, DC, 1983.

References: 1. Aderman et al. 1982, 4, pp. 381–383; Butler 1962, p. 19; Butler 1974, p. 23; Myers 1974, p. 23.
JAA

47

48

*his little dog.*

*Washington Irving.
from life.     July
1848*

### 49. "Sunnyside" Washington Irving's House on the Hudson

Felix Octavius Carr Darley (1822–1888)
Tarrytown, New York, July 24, 1848
Wash on paper
9⅜ x 13⅜"
23.8 x 34.0 cm
SS.79.31

Irving is depicted as a country gentleman standing before Sunnyside in this drawing by Felix O.C. Darley. The picture was executed in 1848, a year after the completion of the tower, which is visible at the viewer's right. Designed to accommodate additional guest rooms and servant's quarters, the tower also added to the aesthetic appeal of the house. Irving's inspiration had been the Moorish-inspired towers that he had seen on his travels while minister to the Spanish court. Many of his friends, however, referred to the steep-pitched roof as the "Pagoda."

Darley's portrayal of Irving next to his cottage is rare. The only other visual record of Irving posed outside of Sunnyside is a somewhat stiff stereoscopic slide of the writer seated in the entryway. Darley's quick sketch of Irving standing before the house, casually dressed, captures the comfort that life at Sunnyside afforded him. "Here," he wrote in 1850, "I hope to pass the handful of years I can yet count upon winding up my varied and precarious life....It is not often that one who has been so much a wanderer and at times been so buffeted by fortune, reaches such a quiet haven at last."[1]

Provenance: Bland Gallery, Inc., New York City, 1946.

References: 1. Aderman et al. 1982, 4, p. 237; Butler 1983, p. 215; Butler 1974, p. 35; Groce and Wallace, 1957, p. 165; Ethel King, *Darley, The Most Popular Illustrator of His Time*, Brooklyn, NY: Theo. Gaus' Sons, 1964; Frank Weintenkamf, "F.O.C. Darley, American Illustrator," *Art Quarterly* 10 (Spring 1947), pp. 100–113.
JAA

50. *Washington Irving* (1783–1859)

William Henry Powell (1823–1879)
New York City, 1855
Watercolor on ivory
4⅝ x 3⅝″
11.8 x 9.2 cm
SS.64.47

Sunnyside's interiors welcomed some of the most noteworthy figures of the mid-nineteenth century. Like the building's façade and surroundings, the interiors reflected Irving's taste. Many of his letters to Harvey, who aided in the expansion of the cottage, attest to the author's contributions. Irving included sketches in his correspondence, describing types of molding to be used, window configurations, and even a wallpaper treatment.

This miniature of Irving by artist William Henry Powell, thought to be one of the few visual records of the cottage's interior during the author's lifetime, is inscribed on its cardboard backing "Washington Irving/ Sunnyside 1855/W.H. Powell/N.Y. City." Irving is shown in one of the seating bays of cottage. The view from the window suggests that Irving was seated at the southern window of either his study or dining room.

Information recorded on the reverse of the miniature contradicts the official history of the image. William Powell was commissioned to do a posthumous portrait of Irving for Goupil and Company. That completed work, measuring 86 x 58 inches was similar in composition to this miniature. It was later engraved by Paul LePrix in 1863. A pamphlet promoting the sale of the print states that the large portrait was based on the Mathew Brady Studio daguerreotype and a bust of Irving, as well as Powell's personal remembrance of the author. No mention was made of a portrait by Powell taken from life. However, the inscription "Washington Irving/ Sunnyside 1855/W.H. Powell/N.Y. City" supports the theory that this miniature was done from life. The architecture of the window surround, the grained treatment of the woodwork, and the curule-style stool included at the viewer's left are known to have existed at Sunnyside during Irving's lifetime.

Historic Hudson Valley also owns an oil-on-canvas version of this portrait, 19½ x 14½ inches in size, which includes a bookcase to the sitter's right. This feature may have been added to symbolize Irving's significant role in the development and promotion of American literature.

Provenance: M. Collins

References: *American Historical Portraits, Property of the Estate of the Late Hiram Burlingham*, New York: Anderson Galleries, 1934, p. 48, no. 76; Butler 1974, p. 24; Butler 1983, p. 219; Groce and Wallace 1957, p. 513; New York *Herald Tribune*, April 3, 1948, p. 15; William Henry Powell, *Full-Length Portrait of Washington Irving in His Library at Sunnyside*, New York: Groupil and Company, 1860, pp. 3–4.
JAA

## 51. *Leisure Hours*

Evie A. Todd
New York, 1864–1868
Ink wash on paper, leather binding
12⅜ x 10⁵⁄₁₆ x 1½"
31.4 x 26.2 x 3.8 cm
W247

Little is known about Evie A. Todd, the amateur artist who compiled these renderings of buildings and landscapes dating between February, 1864 and May, 1868. She resided in Irvington, New York, and must have been familiar with the Irving's cottage nearby. The four views shown here—*The Entrance, The Cottage–Northview, The Cottage–Southview, The Ice House*—were completed in March, 1866, seven years after Irving's death. They illustrate both the charm of the physical landscape and, more significantly, the role that Sunnyside—the house and grounds—played in nineteenth-century America.

Todd's drawings also record a number of Irving's interesting additions to the landscape and house. The "Ice House" was designed to look like a small country church overlooking the Hudson River. The drawing of the entrance shows a simple metal fence of intersecting horizontal and vertical rods. This fence was designed by Irving to be portable so that it could be shifted about the property when needed. The drawing entitled *The Cottage–Northview* reveals one of numerous skylights incorporated into the roof. Increasing the light in the attic and second-floor rooms, these glass panes were probably inspired by interiors seen by Irving in Europe.

Todd's book, perhaps a record of her travels, was bound in Paris. It also includes drawings of Niagara Falls, the mountains of Colorado, Jefferson's Monticello, and the English countryside.

Provenance: Old Print Shop, New York City, 1956.

References: Butler 1974, p. 65.
JAA

# Sunnyside.

## MARCH 1866

The Entrance

The Cottage – North view

The Cottage – South view

The Ice-house

## 52. *Sunnyside from the Hudson*

Unknown artist
America, 1860–1880
Oil on canvas
24¹/₁₆ x 34¹/₁₆"
61.1 x 86.5 cm
SS.64.542

Prior to the arrival of the railroad in 1847, the cottage sat on a small peninsula jutting into the Hudson. The construction of the Hudson River Railroad (later the New York Central) altered the shoreline, making Irving's private cove landlocked. Irving responded to this intrusion by saying "if the garden of Eden were now on Earth, they would not hesitate to run a railroad through it."[1] He wished that he had "been born when the world was finished[2]" and not in the process of being made.

Beyond his expressed frustration regarding the railroad's construction, Irving did achieve some benefits. The railroad provided a $3,500 adjustment to Irving, which helped with the concurrent expansion of the cottage, mainly the construction of the Spanish tower. The railroad also provided Irving with a more direct route to New York City.

This painting was undoubtedly inspired by a similar rendering that appeared in *Frank Leslie's Illustrated Newspaper* of March 31, 1860.[3]

Provenance: J. Watson, 1943.

Exhibitions: "Time, Man and the River," Hudson River Museum, Yonkers, NY, 1977; "The Catskills: Painters, Writers, and Tourists in the Mountains 1820–1895," Hudson River Museum of Westchester, Yonkers, NY, 1988–1989.

References: 1., 2. Harold Dean Cater, *Washington Irving and Sunnyside*, Tarrytown, NY: Sleepy Hollow Restorations, 1957, pp. 24, 31; 3. *Frank Leslie's Illustrated Newspaper*, 31 March 1860, p. 274; Joseph T. Butler, "Washington Irving, Romanticism, and Sunnyside: Part I," *Connoisseur* 167 (January 1968), pp. 51–57; Butler 1974, p. 5; Butler 1983, p. 205; Irving 1864, 4, pp. 36–38; Keller 1976, p. 158; Myers, 1974, p. 113.
JAA

### 53. *Sunnyside*

Unknown artist
America, 1850–1870
Oil on canvas
21½ x 26½"
54.6 x 67.3 cm
SS.77.1
Gift of Harry T. Peters, Jr.

Sunnyside is shown from the southeast, the approach most often used by visitors. An elderly gentleman seated on a bench (possibly a reference to Irving), a flowering garden, and sailing ships in the background are combined to present an idyllic image of the "little snuggery."

This painting may have served as the source for the successful Currier and Ives print, which is almost identical to it, or, more likely, was copied from it.[1] The print remained popular with the public throughout most of the nineteenth century.

Provenance: Harry T. Peters, New York City; Harry T. Peters, Jr., Orange, VA, 1976.

Exhibition: "Currier and Ives and the New York Scene," Museum of the City of the New York, 1938.

References: 1. Harry T. Peters, *Currier & Ives, Printmakers to the American People*, 2 vols., reprint, New York: Arno Press, 1976, 1, no. 4184, 2, pl. 252; Butler 1976, fig. 29; Butler 1983, p. 202.
JAA

## 54. Vase

Odell and Booth Brothers pottery
(1881–1887)
Tarrytown, NY, c. 1883
Earthenware
13⅛ x 8½ x 4″
33.3 x 21.6 x 10.2 cm
SS.64.152
Gift of Mrs. Worcester R. Warren

The popularity of Sunnyside, both during and after Irving's lifetime, is exemplified by this piece of art pottery by the short-lived firm of Odell and Booth Brothers. The house, as illustrated through numerous prints and photographs and as described in magazine articles and books, came to symbolize and define the ideal of "home" for many Americans. Oliver Wendell Holmes believed that Irving's house along the Hudson was the most recognizable home in America, next to George Washington's Mount Vernon.

The vase is inscribed on the reverse, "Sunnyside Home of Washington Irving." It is signed "Taunay" and marked "O. & BB." Taunay was a French decorator employed by the pottery.

Provenance: Leslie V. Case Collection, Tarrytown, NY; Mrs. Worcester R. Warner, Tarrytown, NY.

References: Edwin A. Barber, *The Pottery and Porcelain of the United States, an historical review of American Ceramic Art from the earliest times to the present day,* 3d edition, 1909, reprint (combined with *Marks of American Potters, 1904*), New York: Feingold & Lewis, 1976, p. 308; Butler 1983, p. 259; Paul Evans, *Art Pottery of the United States, An Encyclopedia of Producers and Their Marks,* Hanover, PA: Everybody's Press, 1974, p. 202; Kirsten H. Keen, *American Art Pottery 1875–1930,* Wilmington, DE: Delaware Art Museum, 1978, figs. 12, 13; Leigh Keno, "Odell and Booth Brothers, Art Potters of Tarrytown," *Art & Antiques* 3 (March-April 1980), pp. 96–101.

JAA

## 55. *Sunnyside with Picnickers*

John Henry Hill (1839–1922)
New York, 1878
Watercolor on paper
19½ x 29″
49.5 x 73.7 cm
SS.79.4
Gift in memory of Mrs. John D.
Rockefeller, Jr., by her children

Sunnyside remained a popular gathering place for visitors even after Irving's death in 1859. Both family and admirers of the famous writer saw the cottage as somewhat of a shrine. Rooms on the main floor of the house, including Irving's study, were preserved for many years as he had known them. Travelers to the region often walked about the grounds, admiring the special world Irving had created along the banks of the Hudson.

This watercolor by artist John Henry Hill includes children from a neighboring estate playing on the lawn, with the house serving as a backdrop.

One of a family of painters from across the river in Nyack, New York, Hill was a great admirer of John Ruskin and the pre-Raphaelite movement. This work attests to Hill's attention to natural detail.

Provenance: Downtown Gallery, New York City; Mrs. John D. Rockefeller, Jr., New York City, 1948.

Exhibition: "Drawings of the Hudson River School," The Brooklyn Museum, NY, 1969; "The New Path: Ruskin and the American Pre-Raphaelites," The Brooklyn Museum, NY, 1985.

References: Butler 1974, fig. 28; Butler 1983, p. 221; Linda S. Ferber and William H. Gerdts, *The New Path: Ruskin and the American Pre-Raphaelites*, Brooklyn, NY: The Brooklyn Museum, 1985, p. 167–169; Groce and Wallace 1957, p. 316; Terry B. Morton, "What good is a Poet's House?" *Historic Preservation* 12 (1960), pp. 44–51, illus. cover; *M. & M. Karolik Collection of American Water Colors & Drawings 1800–1875*, 2 vols., Boston: Museum of Fine Arts, 1962, 1, pp. 188–189; Jo Miller, *Drawings of the Hudson River School*, Brooklyn, NY: The Brooklyn Museum, 1969, p. 88, illus. fig. 74; Theodore E. Stebbins, Jr., *American Master Drawings and Water Colors, A History of Works on Paper from Colonial Times to the Present*, New York: Harper and Row, 1976, fig. 122.
JAA

# Key to Abbreviated References

*Aderman et al. 1978–1982*

Ralph M. Aderman, Herbert L. Kleinfield, and Jenifer S. Banks, editors. *Washington Irving: Letters.* 4 vols. Boston: Twayne Publishers, 1978–1982.

*Bowden 1981*
Mary W. Bowden. *Washington Irving.* Boston: Twayne Publishers, 1981.

*Butler 1967*
Joseph T. Butler. *The Family Collections at Van Cortlandt Manor.* Tarrytown, NY: Sleepy Hollow Restorations, 1967.

*Butler 1974*
Joseph T. Butler. *Washington Irving's Sunnyside.* Tarrytown, NY: Sleepy Hollow Restorations, 1974.

*Butler 1983*
Joseph T. Butler. *Sleepy Hollow Restorations: A Cross-Section of the Collection.* Tarrytown, NY: Sleepy Hollow Restorations, 1983.

*Callow 1967*
James I. Callow. *Kindred Spirits: Knickerbocker Writers and American Artists. 1807–1855.* Chapel Hill, NC: University of North Carolina Press, 1967.

*Cunningham 1843*
Allan Cunningham. *The Life of Sir David Wilkie.* London: John Murray, 1843.

*Dunlap 1969*
William Dunlap. *A History of the Rise and Progress of the Arts of Design in the United States.* Reprint. New York: Dover, 1969.

*Faison and Mills 1982*
S. Lane Faison, Jr. and Sally Mills. *Hudson Valley People, Albany to Yonkers, 1700–1900.* (Exhibition held 16 April–6 June 1982.) Poughkeepsie, NY: Vassar College Art Gallery, 1982.

*Groce and Wallace 1957*
George C. Groce and David H. Wallace. *The New-York Historical Society's Dictionary of Artists in America 1564–1860.* New Haven: Yale University Press, 1957.

*Harvey 1850*
George Harvey. *A Descriptive Pamphlet of the Original Drawings of American Scenery; Under Various Atmospheric Effects of Storm and Calm; of Sunshine and Shade; Together with Sketches of the Homes and Haunts of the British Poets, to which is Prefixed, A Brief Autobiography of the Artist's Life.* London: W. J. Golbourn, 1850.

*...illustrated by Darley 1978*
*...illustrated by Darley: May 4–June 18, 1978. An exhibition of original drawings by the American book illustrator Felix Octavius Carr Darley, 1822–1888.* Wilmington: Delaware Art Museum, 1978.

*Irving 1862–1864*
Pierre M. Irving. *The Life and Letters of Washington Irving.* 4 vols. New York: G. P. Putnam, 1862–1864.

*Irving 1982*
Washington Irving. *Life of Washington*. 5 vols. Boston: Twayne Publishers, 1982.

*Keller 1976*
Allan Keller. *Life Along the Hudson*. Tarrytown, NY: Sleepy Hollow Restorations, 1976.

*Knoedler 1946*
*Washington Irving and His Circle*. A Loan Exhibition observing the Restoration of "Sunnyside," October 8 through October 26, 1946. New York: M. Knoedler and Company, 1946.

*Koke 1982*
Richard J. Koke. *American Landscape and Genre Paintings in the New-York Historical Society: A Catalogue of the Collection, Including Historical, Narrative, and Marine Art*. New York: The New-York Historical Society and Boston: G. K. Hall & Co., 1982.

*Leslie 1860*
Charles Robert Leslie. *Autobiographical Recollections*. Boston: Ticknor and Fields, 1860.

*McFarland 1979*
James McFarland. *Sojourners*. New York: Atheneum, 1979.

*Myers 1976*
Andrew B. Myers, editor. *A Century of Commentary on the Works of Washington Irving*. Tarrytown, NY: Sleepy Hollow Restorations, 1976.

*Myers 1974*
Andrew B. Myers, editor. *The Worlds of Washington Irving, 1783–1859. From an exhibition of rare book and manuscript materials in the special collections of The New York Public Library*. Tarrytown, NY: Sleepy Hollow Restorations, 1974.

*Myers 1972*
Andrew B. Myers., editor. *Washington Irving: A Tribute*. Tarrytown, NY: Sleepy Hollow Restorations, 1972.

*Prown 1956*
Jules David Prown. "Washington Irving's Interest in Art and His Influence Upon American Painting." Unpublished M.A. thesis, University of Delaware, 1956.

*Sokol 1973*
David M. Sokol. *John Quidor: Painter of American Legend*. Wichita, KS: Wichita Art Museum, 1973.

*Wagenknecht 1962*
Edward Wagenknecht. *Washington Irving: Moderation Displayed*. New York: Oxford University Press, 1962.

*Williams 1935*
Stanley T. Williams. *The Life of Washington Irving*. 2 vols. New York: Oxford University Press, 1935.

# Artists' and Makers' Index

# Acknowledgments

Much of what is known about the life and work of Washington Irving is due to the research and writings of Dr. Andrew B. Myers, now retired from Fordham University. Dr. Myers served this institution for many years as consultant on Irving and his invaluable contributions are gratefully acknowledged here.

Thanks also to those mentioned below who have either contributed to the scholarship concerning Washington Irving or to the realization of this exhibition and catalog:

James Abbott, Agnes Ball, Linda Blum, Elinor Bradshaw, Kathleen Casey, Constance Collins, Nancy Dana Gold, Jacquetta Haley, Mary Means Huber, Kathleen Eagen Johnson, Nancy Kraybill, Sharon La Comb, Elizabeth Betts Leckie, Lee Livney, Susan Gangwere McCabe, Jean Monahan, Alissa Ross, and Patricia Smith.

JOSEPH T. BUTLER

# Photography Credits

Jim Frank: 8, 12, 13, 20, 34, 35 (top and bottom), 36, 37 (top), 38 (top and bottom), 39, 40, 44, 45, 47, 48, 60, 61, 73 (bottom), 75 (top and bottom), 79 (top), 80, 83, 86–87, 91 (bottom), 121.

Martin Friedman: 53, 63, 73 (top), 101, 102–103, 104, 113, 117, 118.

Donald O. Goetze: 26, 27, 59 (bottom), 81, 99 (top), 115 (top).

Wallace McFall: 23, 33, 37 (bottom), 41, 42, 43, 46, 99 (bottom), 105, 125.

Thurman Rotan: 10, 14–15, 18, 25, 36, 37 (top), 47, 51, 55 (top and bottom), 57 (top and bottom), 59 (top), 65, 69, 71 (top and bottom), 77, 79 (bottom), 83, 89, 91 (top), 92, 93, 95, 99, 107, 109, 111, 115 (bottom), 116–117, 119, 122, 124, 127.